THEY NEVER SAID IT

THEY NEVER SAID IT

❀❀❀❀❀❀❀

A Book of Fake Quotes, Misquotes,
and Misleading Attributions

Paul F. Boller, Jr.
John George

BARNES
&NOBLE
BOOKS
NEW YORK

This edition published by Barnes & Noble, Inc.,
by arrangement with Oxford University Press, Inc.

1993 Barnes & Noble Books

ISBN 1-56619-105-X

Printed and bound in the United States of America

M 9 8 7 6 5 4 3 2

For Treva   JOHN
For Don Worcester   PAUL

Preface

Using quotations is a time-honored practice. There have always been people who liked to liven up what they were saying with appropriate statements from the writings of others. This was true even in ancient times; Plato used quotations freely, and Cicero's letters are full of quotations. Today, however, quotations tend to be polemical rather than decorative. People use them to prove points rather than to provide pleasure. As a forensic device, quote-using has become practically indispensable to teachers, preachers, politicians, educators, columnists, editorial writers, commentators, and panelists who are called upon—or who go out of their way—to discuss political and social issues in public. What has been called "quotemanship" (or "quotesmanship")—the use and abuse of quotations for partisan purposes—has during the past few decades become a highly refined art in this country.

Quotemanship, like Stephen Potter's one-upmanship, involves gambits and ploys and countergambits and tricks and traps and ruses and ambuscades. Quotemen (and quotewomen) do not simply quote; they quote in order to score points, usually of a political nature, and thereby throw their opponents off balance. Sometimes they merely quote a highly esteemed authority—Jefferson, Lincoln, Emerson—in order to bolster their own position. Other times they do much better than this: they dig up a statement which their opponent once made that clearly supports their own particular position. And if they are really lucky, they may be able to come up with some kind of *gaffe*—a fatuous remark or statement revealing ignorance or prejudice—that casts doubt on their opponent's honesty, integrity, and good judgment. Looking for *gaffes* has become a major feature of recent American presidential campaigns.

But some quoters are not satisfied with gaffemanship; nor do they regard themselves as bound by the customary rules of civilized discourse. They engage in what writer Milton Mayer once called "contextomy": cutting a statement out of context (e.g., John Adams on religion) in order to give a completely misleading impression of what some famous person believes. And some polemicists go even farther than this; they deliberately make up statements out of whole cloth for use in advancing their own position and damaging that of their opponents. In the 1950s Wisconsin Senator Joseph R. McCarthy became a master of the contrived quotation. On March 30, 1950, he delivered a long attack in the Senate on the Far Eastern policies of the Roosevelt and Truman administrations, during the course of which he tried to discredit Owen Lattimore (who had been director of Pacific Operations, Office of War Information, during World War II) by reading the following statement from a letter he said Lattimore had written in 1943: "Fire from the O.W.I. any man who is loyal to Chiang, and hire individuals who are loyal to the Communist government." But when his fellow Senators asked to see the letter from which he read his quotation, McCarthy said it was "secret." It turned out that he had simply made up the quote on the spot.

Few quote-mongers are as audacious as Senator McCarthy. Most of them invent their quotations in the quiet of their offices or the shelter of their homes rather than in public. But many of them are just as unscrupulous as the Wisconsin Senator. They enjoy putting words into the mouths of famous people, particularly the long-departed, and then citing these words with an air of authority in their earnest little books, pamphlets, newspapers, magazines, and leaflets. Some of the quotes they make up pass into general circulation and are accepted as authentic by the general public. On occasion even serious scholars and conscientious public officials are taken in by them. In September 1985, President Ronald Reagan made innocent use of an old-time fake quote from Lenin in one of his speeches: "First, we will take eastern Europe, then the masses of Asia, then we will encircle the United States which will be the last bastion of capitalism. We will not have to attack. It will fall like an overripe fruit into our hands." Lenin was a zealot when it came to communism, but he was not stupid. And he simply wasn't given to making fatuous remarks like the one about overripe fruit.

The overripe-fruit statement is just one of a host of phony Lenin quotes that have been making the rounds in this country since the Bolshevik Revolution of 1917. But there are also plenty of fake Lincoln quotes in circulation. And there are spurious quotes, too, from Franklin, Washington, and other notables that turn up periodically in books, pamphlets, magazine articles, and public adresses. Some of these quotes, to be sure, originated in misunderstanding or carelessness in reporting; and some of them (like the quotes about George Washington's piety) in wishful thinking rather than in malice. And there are plenty of harmless concoctions (we have included a few) which have been put into the mouths of celebrities, mainly show people, by publicity agents and gossip columnists, in order to jazz up their public images. Harmless, too, are the misattributed quotes (like the one about the weather that Charles Dudley Warner, not Mark Twain, really made), and the misquotes (like Churchill's "blood, sweat, and tears"), which are sometimes improvements on the original. But a lot of the phony quotes assembled here were deliberately manufactured with malice prepense; the quote-maker simply wrote out a statement of his own, put quotation marks around it, and attributed it to someone else. And his aim was to mislead, not amuse.

When Emperor Charlemagne died in 814 and no comet appeared, chroniclers simply invented one and inserted it into history, for comets in those days were closely associated with the deaths of great leaders. Twentieth-century quote-mongers are like the ninth-century comet-makers; they dream up things that never happened but which they think should have and then insert them into history. For some reason, American reactionaries have gone in more for quote-making than American radicals. This is possibly because the former feel more of a need for authoritative quotes than the latter. Radicals have plenty of quotations from Karl Marx, anyway, and probably see no need to add to the Marxist treasure-house. Extreme rightists in America have a real problem, in any case; they would like to cite the Founding Fathers, but rarely find what they want in Franklin, Washington, and Jefferson. Hence the quote-faking.

In the present book, we have made a careful distinction between the misquotations and misattributions (usually unintentional) and the deliberate forgeries. We have also tried, where possible, to track down the origin of the spurious quotes contained in the book and give evidence for their inauthenticity. It is difficult, of course, to prove negatives; but some of the statements attributed to, say, Washington and Franklin, are so preposterous that they are self-evidently apocryphal. But sometimes it takes hours of research in the collected works of noted writers to demonstrate that certain quotations have been concocted out of thin air. It is amusing, in a way, to find the sources becoming vaguer and vaguer as one follows the trail of a quotation that was improbable at the outset. Quote-makers haven't made it easy for the conscientious.

It is doubtless too much to expect that a book like *They Never Said It* will succeed in putting an end to the concocting of phony statements for polemical purposes. It may, though, be of real value to people who resent being taken in by the quote-fakers in our midst. John Ruskin once lamented the "splendid mendacity of mankind." When it comes to quotations, the mendacity has tended to be sleazy rather than splendid. It's amusing when fundamentalists put a repudiation of evolution in the mouth of Charles Darwin as he lay dying. But there is nothing funny about the anti-Catholic and anti-Semitic sentiments which hate-mongers have invented and put in the mouth of the prejudice-free Benjamin Franklin.

Texas Christian University Paul F. Boller, Jr.
Fort Worth, Texas

Central State University John H. George
Edmond, Oklahoma

A Note to Our Readers

We would appreciate knowing about any quotational curiosities and spuriosities which we have missed. Please send material to either Paul F. Boller, Jr., History Department, Texas Christian University, Fort Worth, Texas 76129, or to John George, Department of Political Science, Central State University, Edmond, Oklahoma 73060.

Contents

Lincoln, Abraham

THEY NEVER SAID IT

❀ Adams, John (1735–1826)

NO-RELIGION QUOTE "This would be the best of all possible worlds if there were no religion in it."

Although atheistic organizations like to make use of this no-religion remark in order to portray the second President of the United States as a freethinker, they are quoting out of context. Adams did indeed make the statement, but only to repudiate it. In a letter to Thomas Jefferson about religion on April 19, 1817, he mentioned reading some polemical books that reminded him of the way his boyhood minister, Lemuel Bryant, and his Latin schoolmaster, Joseph Cleverly, used to argue *ad nauseam* about religion, and he told Jefferson: "Twenty times, in the course of my late reading, have I been on the point of breaking out, 'this would be the best of all possible worlds, if there were no religion in it!!!!' But in this exclamation, I should have been as fanatical as Bryant or Cleverly. Without religion, this world would be something not fit to be mentioned in public company—I mean hell."[1]

❀ Addison, Joseph (1672–1719)

HESITATES-LOST QUOTE "He who hesitates is lost."

The original line in British writer Addison's play, *Cato* (1713), was: "The woman that deliberates is lost."[2]

3

❀ Allen, Ethan (1738–1789)

IN-THE-NAME-OF-JEHOVAH QUOTE   "In the name of the great Jehovah and the Continental Congress!"

At dawn on May 10, 1775, when Revolutionary patriot Ethan Allen called on the British to surrender Fort Ticonderoga, at the head of Lake Champlain, the British commandant wanted to know by what authority he was invading the King's property. "In the name of the Great Jehovah and the Continental Congress!" Allen said he replied. But he did not record the exchange until four years later, and his memory seems to have been a bit faulty. It was a junior officer, not the Fort's commandant, to whom he made his surrender demand, and the poor man, roused from sleep by all the noise, came out of his room holding his trousers in his hand. Some of the men who were at the Fort with Allen later said the Vermonter had shouted, "Come out of here, you damned old Rat." Others remembered his exclamation: "Come out of there, you sons of British whores, or I'll smoke you out." Allen was the only one who recalled mentioning the great Jehovah and the Continental Congress, and, as a Vermont historian pointed out, he had a commission from neither one.[3]

❀ Armstrong, Neil (1930–   )

SMALL-STEP QUOTE   "That's one small step for man, one giant leap for mankind."

On July 20, 1969, at 10:56 (E.D.T.), astronaut Neil Armstrong stepped out of the lunar module that had carried him through thousands of miles of space to become the first human being to set foot on the moon. His statement upon that historic occasion was transmitted to earth and heard around the world. But when he got back to earth he discovered he had been misunderstood. "That's one small step for a man," he had announced, "one giant leap for mankind." But because of static, the particle, "a," had been left out of his statement, thus ruining the contrast he had made between one man ("a" man) and all mankind ("man"). Newspapers and the wire services soon reported Armstrong's correction, but the faulty version continues to circulate.[4]

❋ Beria, Lavrenti (1899–1953)

PSYCHOPOLITICS QUOTE "By psychopolitics create chaos. Leave a nation leaderless. Kill our enemies. And bring to Earth, through Communism, the greatest peace Man has ever known."

According to Edward Hunter, author of *Brain-Washing in Red China* (1953), two Englishmen picked up Hunter's term, "brain-washing," and put together a sixty-page booklet they called *Brain-Washing: A Synthesis of the Russian Textbook on Psychopolitics*. In it they featured "An Address by Beria," which contained the psychopolitics statement (once much-loved by the ultra-rightist John Birch Society), and made suggestions for waging psychological warfare against the Western democracies. Beria's address, they said, was delivered at Lenin University in 1936, when Beria was head of the Soviet secret police, and they added that his audience consisted of Soviet-sympathizing American students.

But L. Ron Hubbard, Jr., son of the notorious founder of Scientology, claimed that his father originated the psychopolitics hoax. "Dad wrote every word of it," he insisted. "Barbara Bryan and my wife typed the manuscript off his dictation. . . . Years later they snuck it into the Library of Congress, and somebody else came by and said, 'Lookee, it was found in the Library of Congress!' which is a lot of baloney." John Sanborne, who had edited Hubbard's books since the early 1950s, claimed that he thought up the idea for the book while chatting with the Scientology sage one afternoon. "I suggested it," he later declared. "Just kidding around on his front porch." He was discussing psychiatrists with Hubbard, he said, and suddenly cried: "What we need to do is take over their subject. What we need to put out is a manual of psych-military or something or other . . . as coming from the communists and then put a lot of psychiatry in it." Hubbard took to the idea with zest, rushed from the front porch, and began dictating the book in his office.

Whatever the provenance, the Beria quote first attracted public attention when Congress was considering legislation to provide funds for mental hospitals in the Territory of Alaska. Radical rightist Kenneth Goff (an ex-communist), joined by other far rightists, charged that the Alaskan Mental Health bill was a Communist plot to establish a concentration camp in Alaska for patriotic anti-communists; and to prove his point he distributed copies of the brain-washing manual, with its spurious Beria quote, to Congressmen and other interested parties. The bill finally passed with the support of both the American Medical Association and conservative Republican Senator Barry M. Goldwater of Arizona, but the Beria quote continued circulating. Sometimes it is attributed to Josef Stalin himself.[5]

TEEN-AGERS QUOTE "If we can effectively kill the national pride and patriotism of just one generation, we will have won that country. Therefore we must continue propaganda abroad to undermine the loyalty of citizens in general and of teen-agers in particular."

Like the psychopolitics quote, the Beria statement about teen-agers was popular among ultra-rightists in the 1960s but just as phony. There is no record of any speech made by Beria in which either statement appears.[6]

Bible

CLEANLINESS QUOTE "Cleanliness is next to godliness."

One of the more popular pseudo-Scriptural quotes, the cleanliness admonition, comes, not from the Bible, but from John Wesley, the 18th-century British clergyman who founded Methodism. In a sermon entitled "On Dress," based on a passage in the New Testament, Wesley told his congregation: "Let it be observed, that slovenliness is no part of religion; that neither this nor any text of Scripture condemns neatness of apparel; certainly this is a duty, not a sign. 'Cleanliness is, indeed, next to godliness.'" Wesley was quoting an old proverb which goes back to Phinehas ben-Yair, a Hebrew sage who lived in the latter part of the second century and formulated the famous "ladder to saintliness." Wrote Rabbi Phinehas: "The doctrines of religion are resolved into carefulness; carefulness into vigorousness; vigorousness into guiltlessness; guiltlessness into abstemiousness; abstemiousness into cleanliness; cleanliness into godliness."[7]

FOOLS-RUSH-IN QUOTE "Fools rush in where angels fear to tread."

Many people think this is the Bible, but it's actually Alexander Pope. In *An Essay on Criticism* (1711), the British poet wrote: "For Fools rush in where Angels fear to tread."[8]

GOD-HELPS QUOTE "God helps him who helps himself."

Found nowhere in the Bible, this popular self-help aphorism seems to have its origin in the writings of the sixth-century Greek sage Aesop. His fable "Hercules and the Wagoner" features the words, "Help when you pray or prayer is vain," or, in a more prolix translation: ". . . never more pray to me for help, until you have done your best to help yourself, or depend upon it you will henceforth pray in vain."[9]

PRIDE QUOTE   "Pride goeth before a fall."

What Proverbs says is : "Pride goeth before destruction, and an haughty spirit before a fall."[10]

SAFETY-IN-NUMBERS QUOTE   "There's safety in numbers."

"Where no counsel is, the people fall," says Proverbs; "but in the multitude of counselors *there is* safety."[11]

SPARE-THE-ROD QUOTE   "Spare the rod and spoil the child."

It was the English poet Samuel Butler, in *Hudibras* (1664), who wrote: "Then spare the rod and spoil the child." The Bible says, "He that spareth his rod hateth his son" (Proverbs 13:24) and "Foolishness is bound in the heart of a child; but the rod of correction shall drive it far from him" (Proverbs 22:15).[12]

THE WIND QUOTE   "Who hath seen the wind?"

This query does not come from the Bible, but from some lines by the nineteenth-century English poet Christina G. Rossetti:

> Who has seen the wind?
> Neither you nor I:
> But when the trees bow down their heads
> The wind is passing by.[13]

✿ Bogart, Humphrey (1899–1957)

PLAY-IT-AGAIN QUOTE   "Play it again, Sam."

The actual line in Warner Brothers's famous World War II movie, *Casablanca* (1943), is, "Play it, Sam. Play 'As Time Goes By.'" And it's uttered by Ingrid Bergman (Ilse), not by Humphrey Bogart (Rick), to "pianist"-singer Dooley

Wilson (Sam). But Sam doesn't really play it; he just sings it. For Wilson couldn't play the piano, and the song's accompaniment was dubbed in.[14]

TENNIS QUOTE "Tennis, anyone?"

Although *Bartlett's Familiar Quotations* lists this as a Bogart quote, the popular actor denied he ever uttered it in play, movie, or in person.[15]

❀ Boyer, Charles (1897–1978)

CASBAH QUOTE "Come with me to the Casbah."

In *Algiers,* an American movie released in 1938 which featured a steamy romance between Charles Boyer (playing Pepe, a French crook who lives lavishly in the Casbah) and Hedy Lamarr (a beautiful Parisienne visiting Algiers), Boyer supposedly says this to Lamarr early in the picture. But he didn't; nor did he say it in any other movie or play he was in. For years, however, people who got fun out of doing Boyer-the-great-lover imitations made constant use of the corybantic quote, even though Boyer insisted it was a fabrication of his press agent.[16]

❀ Brezhnev, Leonid (1906–1982)

TREASURE-HOUSES-OF-WEST QUOTE "Our aim is to gain control of the two great treasure houses on which the West depends. . . . The energy treasure house of the Persian Gulf and the mineral treasure house of Central and Southern Africa."

Leonid Brezhnev, General Secretary of the Central Committee of the Soviet Union from 1966 until 1982, was supposed to have made the treasure-houses statement at a secret meeting of the Warsaw Pact nations in either 1968 or in 1973. But Brezhnev-quoters failed to explain how they happened to learn about a statement made at a vaguely dated secret meeting of Warsaw Pact nations. According to the Library of Congress's Research Service there is "no direct documentation" for the quotation. There are several versions of the statement, which has been traced to a Czechoslovakian defector named Jan Sejna, and the one cited here appeared in an extreme-rightist magazine, *The American Sentinel*, in 1982.[17]

✻ Burke, Edmund (1729–1797)

INDICT-A-WHOLE-PEOPLE QUOTE   "You cannot indict a whole people."

In a speech in Parliament on March 22, 1775, entitled, "On Moving His Resolution for Conciliation with the Colonies," Burke declared: "I do not know the method of drawing up an indictment against an whole people." But he was soon being quoted as saying, "You cannot indict a whole people," and the pithier statement became standard.[18]

TRIUMPH-OF-EVIL QUOTE   "The only thing necessary for evil to triumph is for good men to do nothing."

The much-quoted triumph-of-evil statement appeared in the 14th edition of *Bartlett's Familiar Quotations* (1968), with a letter Burke wrote William Smith on January 9, 1795, given as the source. But the letter to Smith was dated January 29, 1795, and it said nothing about the triumph of evil. When *New York Times* columnist William Safire asked Emily Morison Beck, editor of the 15th edition of *Bartlett's*, about the source, she acknowledged that she hadn't located the statement in Burke's writings "so far," but suggested it might be a paraphrase of something Burke said in a speech he gave in

Parliament, "Thoughts on the Cause of the Present Discontents," on April 23, 1770: "When bad men combine, the good must associate; else they will fall, one by one, an unpitied sacrifice in a contemptible struggle." Safire thought her suggestion was a "pretty long stretch," but she included it in her introduction to the new edition of *Bartlett's*.[19]

Butler, Samuel (1612–1680)

MAN-CONVINCED-AGAINST-HIS-WILL QUOTE "A man convinced against his will is of the same opinion still."

What the 17th-century British poet actually wrote in his mock epic, *Hudibras* (1664), was: "He that complies against his will is of his own opinion still." It would be extremely difficult to *convince* a person of something against his or her will.[20]

Cagney, James (1899–1986)

RAT QUOTE "You dirty rat!"

Film star James Cagney, famous for his gangster roles, denied ever having said any such thing in any of his seventy-odd movies.[21]

Cambronne, Pierre Jacques Etienne (1770–1842)

GUARD QUOTE *"La Guarde meurt mais ne se rend pas"* (The Guards die but do not surrender).

When the English called on Baron de Cambronne of Napoleon's army to surrender at Waterloo in 1815, a French journalist named Rougement, who had a gift for phrase-making,

reported that Cambronne exclaimed: *"La Guarde meurt mais
ne se rend pas."* But the Baron didn't die; he was taken pris-
oner. And what he really said, he insisted, was, *"Merde,"* an
excrementitious word that came to be called *"le mot Cambronne"* for a time in France. To the end of his life Cambronne denied having uttered the *La-Guarde-meurt* words,
but they were put on a Cambronne statue in his hometown,
Nantes, after his death and soon passed into English and other
languages.[22]

❀ Carlyle, Thomas (1795–1881)

GENIUS QUOTE   "Genius is an infinite capacity for taking
pains."

The great 19th-century British writer didn't say exactly this
in his multi-volumed life of Frederick the Great. He praised
Frederick for working hard to put his finances and administration in order during the first ten years of his reign, and
then observed: "The good plan itself, this comes not of its
own accord; it is the fruit of genius (which means transcen-
dent capacity of taking trouble, first of all). . . ."[23]

❀ Cervantes, Miguel de (1547–1616)

STREETS-OF-BY-AND-BY QUOTE   "Along the streets of by-and-by,
we come to the house of Never."

In June 1969, New York Congressman Emanuel Celler, to
bolster his contention that any delay in extending the voting-
rights act might be dangerous, quoted Cervantes as having
said: "Along the streets of by-and-by, we come to the house
of Never." But research revealed that the actual quote was,
"in the street of the by-and-by stands the hostelry of never,"
and that it came from a poem by the 19th-century English

writer William Ernest Henley, author of "Invictus." When Celler was challenged as to the authority of his quotation, he insisted that if Cervantes didn't say it, it was the work of an ancient Spanish writer, though possibly not Cervantes. He added that he had traced it back to an anthology published in 1851 when Henley was two years old and that the English poet must himself have borrowed it as an adult.[24]

❀ Chou En-lai (See Zhou En-lai)

❀ Churchill, Winston (1874–1965)

BLOOD-SWEAT-TEARS QUOTE   "I have nothing to offer but blood, sweat, and tears."

When Churchill became Prime Minister of Britain soon after the outbreak of World War II, his first address to the House of Commons on May 13, 1940, contained the sentence: "I have nothing to offer but blood and toil, tears and sweat." When someone later pointed out that Henry James had used a similar phrase in his novel, *The Bostonians* (1886), Churchill said he hadn't read the book and was sure he had made up the phrase himself. He liked the words so much, in fact, that he used them again on several crucial occasions during the war. But the public soon revised the Churchillian phrase, partly because the words, "toil" and "sweat" seemed redundant and partly because the word order sounded a bit awkward. Before long Churchill was being quoted as having said, "blood, sweat, and tears," and the words became famous throughout the world. Today, anyone quoting the original statement would be charged with garbling the quote.[25]

TAX-INTO-PROSPERITY QUOTE   "The idea that a nation can tax itself into prosperity is one of the crudest delusions which has ever befuddled the human mind."

Like many other critics of Federal taxes, President Ronald
Reagan took a liking to the Churchill quote and used it in a
speech on March 9, 1982. But the statement appears nowhere
in any of Churchill's writings.[26]

❀ Cicero, Marcus Tullius (106–43 B.C.)

BUDGET-BALANCING QUOTE   "The budget should be balanced.
The Treasury should be filled. Public debt should be re-
duced. The arrogance of officials should be tempered and
controlled, and assistance to foreign lands should be curtailed
lest we ourselves should become bankrupt. The people should
be forced to work and not depend on government subsis-
tence."

In an editorial on January 15, 1986, the *Kansas City Star*
quoted Cicero at length to bolster its own views about government spending. But the editor gave no source for his quotation and, when pressed to do so by skeptics, was unable to
come up with any documentation. The Cicero statement
sounds more like a disgruntled American critic of the welfare state than the Roman statesman.[27]

❀ Clemens, Samuel Langhorne (See Twain, Mark)

❀ Cohen, Israel

RACIAL-TENSION QUOTE   "We must realize that our party's
most powerful weapon is racial tension. By pounding into
the consciousness of the dark races that for centuries they
have been oppressed by the whites, we can mold them to the
program of the Communist Party. In America we will aim
for subtle victory. While inflaming the Negro minority against

the whites, we will endeavor to instill in the whites a guilt complex for their exploitation of the Negroes. We will aid the Negroes to rise in prominence in every walk of life, in the professions and in the world of sports and entertainment. With this prestige, the Negroes will be able to intermarry with the whites and begin a process which will deliver America to our cause."

During the debate on a civil-rights bill in Congress in June 1957, Mississippi Congressman Thomas G. Abernathy read the above statement, taken from a book entitled *A Racial Program for the Twentieth Century,* allegedly written by Israel Cohen, a leading British Communist, and published in 1912. In August 1958, however, New York's Congressman Abraham J. Multer challenged the authenticity of the quotation. Among other things, he pointed out that there was no Communist Party in Britain in 1912 and that the expression "Communist Party" didn't come into existence until after World War I; that no book with such a title written by Israel Cohen or by anyone else could be located in the Library of Congress or in the British Museum Catalogue of Printed Books; and that there was no record of a Communist named Israel Cohen ever having lived in England.

Congressman Multer also read into the *Congressional Record* an article entitled, "Story of a Phony Quotation—A Futile Effort To Pin It Down—'A Racial Program for the 20th Century' Seems to Exist Only in Somebody's Imagination," appearing in the *Washington Star* for February 18, 1958. After a thorough investigation, according to the article, the *Star* succeeded in tracing the phony quote to Eustace Mullins, Jr., who claimed to have copied it from a Zionist publication while doing research work in the Library of Congress in 1952. But as Multer told Congress: "He was discharged years ago from his probationary job as a photographic aid at the Library of Congress because of his authorship and circulation of violently anti-Semitic articles. Mullins has, apparently, a marked propensity for phony claims and counterfeit creations. Some of his counterfeits include a speech by a non-existent Hungarian rabbi, and a Lizzie Stover College Fund—the fictitious Lizzie Stover being described as the Negro mother of President Eisenhower. Mr. Mullins's literary talents, however, have not been confined to forgeries. In 1952, in his own name, he wrote 'Adolf Hitler: An Appreciation,' for the organ of the fascist National Renaissance Party cited by the House Un-American Activities Committee." Despite the *Washington Star* exposé. the phony quote continued to circulate among bigots in the 1980s.[28]

❀   Colson, Charles (1931–   )

GRANDMOTHER QUOTE   "I would walk over my grandmother if necessary."

In a front-page story about Charles ("Chuck") Colson in October 1971, the *Wall Street Journal* portrayed President Nixon's Special Counsel as a "hatchet man" for the President and quoted a Washington official as saying that "Colson would walk over his own grandmother if he had to." Colson didn't mind being called a hatchet man, and he was amused by the remark about his grandmother; after all, both his grandmothers, he pointed out, had been dead for over a quarter of a century. But when the impression spread that he had made the grandmother remark himself, he strongly denied it. "I never said it," he told reporters.

But the following year the grandmother quote got Colson into trouble. And it was mainly his own fault. In August 1972, he returned to Washington from the Republican convention that renominated Nixon for President to find over half the people on his staff off on a long weekend. He was upset; he was eager to begin working at once on the campaign to re-elect the President. But instead of upbraiding his people, he decided to circulate a memo reminding them of how hard he worked for the President and suggesting they do the same. And, for the fun of it, he added: "Many erroneous things about me have found their way into print lately, but last week's UPI story that I was once reported to have said that 'I would walk over my grandmother if necessary' is absolutely accurate." "Mr. Colson," wailed his secretary, "you don't really want this to go to all the staff, do you?" "Of course, Holly," said Colson. "They'll know most of it is tongue-in-cheek, but it will make the point."

Colson miscalculated. His memo, soon leaked to the *Washington Post,* was picked up by the networks and newspapers across the country, and ended up touching off a torrent of criticism. Mail poured into the White House from angry grandmothers, and Colson's own mother voiced her indignation at her son's remark. Two press conferences were held, moreover, by women calling themselves "Charles Colson's grandmother" and announcing their support for Democratic candidate George McGovern. One of them was a Milwaukee black.[29]

❀ Communist Party Directive (1943)

LABEL-THEM-FASCISTS QUOTE "When certain obstructionists [to Communism] become too irritating, label them, after suitable buildups, as fascist or Nazi or anti-Semitic, and use the prestige of antifascist and tolerance organizations to discredit them. In the public mind constantly associate those who oppose us with those names which already have a bad smell. . . . The association will, after enough repetition, become fact in the public mind. . . . Members and front organizations must continually embarrass, discredit and degrade our critics. Accuse them of being traitors to the war effort, fascists, Red-baiters, peace-destroyers, Quislings, labor-baiters and anti-Semites."

This quote, popular in ultraconservative circles for many years, is almost surely a fake. In 1943 the American Communist Party was supporting the war effort (Russia, after all, was America's ally in World War II) with almost super-patriotic enthusiasm and seeking friendly relations, not ideological quarrels, with American non-Communists. After the war ended and the Cold War began, CP, USA, did indeed call its critics Red-baiters and warmongers, but it is highly unlikely that its leaders needed any kind of special directive to guide their action. Researchers in the Library of Congress have been unable to locate any such "directive"; nor do specialists in Soviet affairs regard it as authentic. Extreme rightists continued to make use of it in the 1980s.[30]

❀ Congreve, William (1670–1729)

MUSIC QUOTE   "Music hath charms to soothe the savage beast."

What British playwright William Congreve actually says in his play *The Mourning Bride* (1697) is: "Music hath charms to soothe a savage breast."[81]

❀ Coolidge, Calvin (1872–1933)

HIRED-THE-MONEY QUOTE   "They hired the money, didn't they?"

When there was a proposal to cancel the World War I debts of the Allied nations to the United States, President Coolidge was said to have snorted: "They hired the money, didn't they?" But Claude M. Fuess, Coolidge's biographer, who worked hard to track down the origin of the statement, finally decided it was inauthentic. "I have tried in vain to ascertain the source of this quotation," he said, "and must, under the circumstances, regard it as belonging to the Coolidge apocrypha." When Mrs. Coolidge was asked about it after her husband's death, she said, "I don't know whether he said it, but it is just what he might have said."[82]

🌼 Darwin, Charles (1809–1882)

WISH-I-HADN'T QUOTE   "How I wish I had not expressed my theory of evolution as I have done."

If anyone believes that Darwin ever said this, he will believe anything—and probably does. But on October 20, 1985, TV evangelist Jimmy Swaggart announced that the great British scientist repudiated his life's work as he lay dying, and that he also asked to read the Bible so he could know Jesus.

Swaggart was not the first to make use of the Darwin deathbed recantation. It's an old fabrication. Shortly after Darwin's death at seventy-four on April 19, 1882, the evangelistic widow of Admiral of the Fleet Sir James Hope, told a gathering of students at Northfield Seminary in Massachusetts that she had visited Darwin in his last hours and found him reading the Epistle to the Hebrews. Darwin, she said, announced that he wished he "had not expressed my theory of evolution as I have done," and he also asked her to get some people together so he could "speak to them of Christ Jesus and His salvation, being in a state where he was eagerly savouring the heavenly anticipation of bliss."

But Darwin's daughter Henrietta vigorously denied that her father ever made such statements. "Lady Hope was not present during his last illness, or any illness," she declared. "I believe he never even saw her, but in any case she had no influence over him in any department of thought or belief. He never recanted any of his scientific views, either then or earlier. . . . The whole story has no foundation whatever." Francis Darwin, who was with his father toward the end, reported that Darwin said, "I am not the least afraid to die," a

few hours before his passing. These seem to have been his last
words.[33]

❀   Devereux, James P. S. (1903–   )

SEND-MORE-JAPS QUOTE   "Send us more Japs!"

At the end of World War II, when Lieutenant-Colonel James
P. S. Devereux returned home after almost four years in a
Japanese prisoner-of-war camp, he was astonished by the tremendous public reception he received wherever he went.
"What did I do?" he wanted to know. "What have you
done?" people exclaimed. "Why you? Because you were not
only the commander of Wake Island but when things were
blackest, when you and your men were hanging by the skin
of your teeth, you sent back that heroic message, 'Send us
more Japs!' Magnificent! It ought to be printed in every
American history, right beside John Paul Jones' 'I have not
yet begun to fight.' "
    Devereux quickly set things straight. He wasn't in com-
mand at Wake Island when the Japanese struck there on December 8, 1941, right after attacking Pearl Harbor; he only
commanded the marine detachment there. More important:
"I did not send any such message. As far as I know, it wasn't
sent at all. None of us was that much of a damn fool. We already had more Japs than we could handle." Apparently an
enterprising journalist put the words in Devereux's mouth
in a Honolulu dispatch dated December 16, a few days before
American forces on Wake were forced to surrender after two
weeks of heroic resistance to the Japanese assault.[34]

❀   Dimitrov, Georgi (1882–1949)

SOVIET-POWER QUOTE   "As Soviet power grows, there will be
a greater aversion to Communist parties everywhere. So we

must practice the technique of withdrawal. Never appear in the foreground; let our friends do the work. We must always remember that one sympathizer is generally worth more than a dozen militant Communists. A university professor, who without being a party member lends himself to the interests of the Soviet Union, is worth more than a hundred men with party cards. A writer of reputation, or a retired general, are worth more than 500 poor devils who don't know any better than to get themselves beaten up by the police. Every man has his value, his merit. The writer who, without being a party member, defends the Soviet Union, the union leader who is outside our ranks but defends Soviet international policy, is worth more than a thousand party members."

According to Eudocio Ravines, a former Peruvian Communist who had once been active in Josef Stalin's Third Communist International (Comintern), Georgi Dimitrov, influential Bulgarian Communist leader in the 1930s, uttered these words at the Lenin School of Political Warfare in 1938. In *The Yenan Way,* published in 1951, Ravines reproduced these words from memory, along with a lot of other lengthy statements by Stalin, Manuilsky, and Zinoviev, without documentation of any kind. The Soviet-power statement, which the American Bar Association cited in a report on Communism in 1958 which was read into the *Congressional Record,* doesn't sound like Dimitrov, who surely didn't think that one fellow-traveling writer or labor leader was "worth more than a thousand party members." In any case, there never was such a place as the Lenin School of Political Warfare.[85]

❀ Disraeli, Benjamin (1804–1881)

DIVIDE-THE-UNITED-STATES-FOR-THE-ROTHSCHILDS QUOTE "Under this roof are the heads of the family of Rothschild—a name famous in every capital of Europe and every division

of the globe. If you like, we shall divide the United States
into two parts, one for you, James, and one for you, Lionel.
Napoleon III will do exactly what and all that I shall advise
him."

In the mid-thirties, the Rev. Charles E. Coughlin, a virulent
anti-Semite, made use of this quote to bolster his claim that
the American Civil War had been fought primarily to rid the
United States of control by Jewish bankers. As his source for
Disraeli's supposed remark to the Rothschilds, he cited John
Reeves's *The Rothschilds,* a book out of print since 1887 and
therefore hard to check. But to Coughlin's chagrin, the *Chicago Daily News* got hold of a copy of the book and reported
that, while the first sentence of Father Coughlin's quote was
accurate, he had made up the rest of it himself. Far from saying anything about dividing the United States up between the
two Rothschild brothers, Disraeli had added, after saying, "a
name famous in . . . every division of the globe": "a family
not more regarded for its riches than esteemed for its honor,
virtues, and public spirit.[36]

JEWS-WANT-TO-DESTROY-CHRISTENDOM QUOTE   "The people of
God co-operate with Communism; the peculiar and chosen
people [the Jews] touch the hand of all the scum and low
castes of Europe. And all this because they want to destroy
. . . Christendom."

This improbable statement by Disraeli about the Jews and
Communism seems first to have appeared in a British publication, *The Church Times,* in 1923, and it turns up again in
the vitriolic vaporings of the Rev. Gerald L. K. Smith, America's professional anti-Semite, during and after World War
II. But Benjamin Disraeli, Britain's prime minister in 1868
and from 1874 until 1880, died in 1881, long before Communism became important in the world. Furthermore, although he was baptized into the Church of England, his father was Jewish, and, according to biographer Robert Blake,

he was "intensely proud of the Jewish ancestry which his less worthy enemies flung in his face. . . ."[37]

❀ Donaldson, Sam (1934–   )

HOLD-ON QUOTE   "Hold on, Mr. President!"

In 1987, Sam Donaldson, AGC's aggressive White House correspondent, published a book entitled *Hold on, Mr. President,* but he denied ever having used the phrase at any of the press conferences of the two Presidents (Jimmy Carter and Ronald Reagan) he covered.[38]

❀ Durocher, Leo (1906–   )

NICE-GUYS QUOTE   "Nice guys finish last."

Leo Durocher, baseball manager of the 1940s and 1950s, may have believed this, but he never put it that way. He always insisted that he made the nice-guys comment about the 1948 New York Giants in these words: "Take a look at them. All nice guys. They'll finish last. Nice guys. Finish last." But the last two sentences were later "run together," giving a new meaning to what the Brooklyn Dodger manager was saying. Sportswriter Jimmy Cannon then picked up the phrase to encapsulate Durocher's philosophy.[39]

❀ Edison, Thomas Alva (1847–1931)

DOCTOR-OF-FUTURE QUOTE   "The Doctor of the Future will give no medicine but will interest his patients in the care of the human frame, in diet, and in the cause and prevention of disease."

The doctor-of-the-future statement is popular with American chiropracters. It appears on their stationery and in frames on the walls of their offices. But it appears nowhere in the writings of the great American inventor. Neither the Palmer Chiropractic College archivist in Davenport, Iowa, nor researchers at the Edison Historical Society could locate it. In the early 1980s the American Chiropractic Association offered a small reward to anyone who could provide the source in Edison's writings, but to date there have been no takers.[40]

❁ Eisenhower, Dwight D. (1890–1969)

BIRCH-SOCIETY QUOTE   "The Birch Society is a good patriotic society. I don't agree with what its founder said about me, but that does not detract from the fact that its membership is comprised of many fine Americans dedicated to the preservation of our libertarian Republic."

During the 1964 presidential campaign, the archconservative John Birch Society placed an advertisement in the *Los Angeles Times* which contained kind words about the JBS from half a dozen national leaders, including the above statement by former President Eisenhower. But since JBS founder Robert Welch had once suggested that Ike was soft on Communism, reporters were suspicious about the quote and sought Ike's reaction to it. In Gettysburg, Pennsylvania, one of Ike's aides told them the quotation was "unauthorized and incorrect." He also said: "Without expressing any approbation whatsoever about the John Birch Society and having expressed specifically his resentment of the despicable and false allegations made by the head of the society, the General, at the same time, has said on occasion that he is quite sure that among its members are many devoted citizens sincerely dedicated to the United States." John H. Rousselot, national public relations director of the JBS, insisted he had heard Ike make the statement quoted in the advertisement during a TV appearance, but few non-Birchers were convinced.[41]

❀ Emerson, Ralph Waldo (1803–1882)

CONSISTENCY QUOTE "Consistency is the hobgoblin of little minds."

The way Emerson put it in his essay, "Self-Reliance," was somewhat different: "A foolish consistency is the hobgoblin of little minds, adored by little statesmen and philosophers and divines."[42]

MOUSETRAP QUOTE "Build a better mousetrap, and the world will beat a path to your door."

In a book by Sarah Yule and Mary Keene, published in 1889, seven years after Emerson's death, appears the statement, supposedly made by Emerson in one of his addresses: "If a man can write a better book, preach a better sermon, or make a better mouse-trap than his neighbor, though he builds his house in the woods, the world will make a beaten path to his door." No source was given for the quote, and it appears nowhere in Emerson's published works. In his journal for 1855, however, Emerson did write something like it: "I trust a good deal to common fame, as we all must. If a man has good corn, or wood, or boards, or pigs, to sell, or can make better chairs or knives, crucibles or church organs, than anybody else, you will find a broad hard-beaten road to his house, though it be in the woods."[43]

❀ Fields, W. C. (1879–1946)

CHILDREN-AND-DOGS QUOTE "Anybody who hates children and dogs can't be all bad."

This is something of a misquote. The original line was: "Anybody who hates dogs and babies can't be all bad." But it wasn't the great comedian who said it. It was Leo Rosten, the humorous writer, who said it when introducing Fields at a dinner.[44]

PHILADELPHIA QUOTE   "On the whole, I'd rather be in Philadelphia."

Fields's supposed epitaph does not appear on the vault housing his ashes. Nor did he think up the line himself. It first appeared as a joke in the magazine *Vanity Fair* in the 1920s, and was assigned to Fields after his death.[45]

✿ Francis I (1494–1547)

ALL-IS-LOST QUOTE   "All is lost save honor."

After losing the Battle of Pavia in 1525, France's Francis I was imprisoned by the victor, Spain's Charles V, and in a letter to his mother, Louise of Savoy, he wrote that "of all things there remains to me only honor and life which is safe." But later historians improved this to read, "All is lost save honor." In 1869, "Robber Baron" Jim Fisk made ironic use of it. After losing an unsavory battle with J. Pierpont Morgan over control of a New York railroad, he exclaimed merrily: "Nothing is lost save honor!"[46]

✿ Franklin, Benjamin (1706–1790)

EXCLUDE-JEWS QUOTE   "In whatever country Jews have settled in any great numbers, they have lowered the moral tone, depreciated the commercial integrity, have segregated themselves, and have not been assimilated, have sneered at and tried to undermine the Christian religion, have built up a state within a state, and have, when opposed, tried to strangle that country to death financially.

"If you do not exclude them from the United States, in the Constitution, in less than 200 years they will have swarmed in such great numbers that they will dominate and devour the land and change our form of government."

Along with the forged document, *The Protocols of the Learned Elders of Zion,* American anti-Semites have been fond of quoting the so-called "Benjamin Franklin Prophecy," with its virulent anti-Jewish statements. During the proceedings of the Constitutional Convention in Philadelphia in the summer of 1787, they claim, Franklin rose at one point to make these statements about the Jews.

The Franklin quote apparently first turned up on February 3, 1934, in William Dudley Pelley's pro-Nazi sheet, *Liberation,* published in Asheville, North Carolina. According to Pelley, it was taken from notes made by Charles Cotesworth Pinckney, delegate to the Constitutional Convention from South Carolina, between sessions of the convention, and it was entitled, "Chit-Chats Around the Table During Intermission." But there is no Pinckney diary, and historian Charles Beard, after a thorough investigation of the "Franklin Prophecy," concluded: "This alleged 'Prophecy' ascribed to Franklin is a crude forgery, and his name should be cleared of the crass prejudice attributed to him. There is in our historical records no evidence whatever of any basis for the falsehood."

Like Washington and Jefferson, Franklin was utterly devoid of religious intolerance and prejudice, and he had the friendliest feelings toward citizens of Jewish faith. On one occasion, when the Hebrew Society of Philadelphia sought to raise money for a synagogue, Franklin signed the petition appealing to "citizens of every denomination" for contributions. Nevertheless, during the 1930s and 1940s, the Franklin forgery was cited time and again in the Nazi press in Germany, broadcast over the Nazi radio, and incorporated

into the Nazi bible, *Handbuch der Judenfrage,* by Theodor
Fritsch. It was popular, too, in neo-Nazi circles in the United
states.[47]

INSIDIOUS-CATHOLICS QUOTE   "I fully agreed with Gen. Washington that we must safeguard this young nation, as yet in
its swaddling clothes, from the insidious influence and im-
penetration of the Roman Catholic Church which pauperizes
and degrades all countries and people over whom it holds
sway."

Franklin was no more a Catholic-hater than he was a Jew-
baiter; he strongly deplored religious hatred in all its forms.
But anti-Catholic bigots in the 1930s and 1940s liked to quote
him on the "insidious influence" of the Roman Catholic
Church. Their source: the non-existent Charles C. Pinckney
diary.[48]

TIGER QUOTE   "Don't unchain the tiger!"

When Thomas Paine completed *Age of Reason* (1794–95),
a Deistic work critical of orthodox Christianity, Benjamin
Franklin is supposed to have written Paine advising against
its publication. "Don't unchain the tiger!" he was quoted by
evangelists like Billy Sunday as having told Paine. But Franklin died in 1790 and Paine didn't begin writing his book
until 1793.[49]

�֍ Frietchie, Barbara (1766?–1862)

SHOOT-IF-YOU-MUST QUOTE   " 'Shoot if you must this old gray
head, but spare your country's flag,' she said."

In July 1863, Mrs. Emma Southworth, popular sentimental
novelist, wrote John Greenleaf Whittier about a dramatic
event one of her neighbors, C. S. Bramsburg, had just related

to her. In September 1862, she told Whittier, when Confederate troops commanded by General Thomas J. ("Stonewall") Jackson entered Frederick, Maryland, all the Union flags were lowered but one. And that defiant one belonged to Barbara Frietchie. Mrs. Frietchie, a ninety-seven-year-old widow, went up to her attic, according to Mrs. Southworth, and, as Confederate forces passed her house, leaned out of the window and proudly displayed the Union flag. And when some of the soldiers fired at it, breaking the flag staff, Mrs. Frietchie quickly grabbed the stump, with the flag still attached, held it out of the window as far as she could, and yelled: "Fire at this old head, then, boys; it is not more venerable than your flag!" At this, Mrs. Southworth said, the Confederates fired no more; and until they evacuated the city a few days later, General Jackson saw to it that his soldiers left her alone.

After reading Mrs. Southworth's letter, Whittier sat down and wrote his famous ballad, "Barbara Frietchie," and when it appeared in the *Atlantic* in October 1863, it was an immediate success. But some people questioned the accuracy of Mrs. Southworth's story; they pointed out that Mrs. Frietchie was bedridden at the time and that she died soon after Jackson left town. A Mrs. Mary Quantrell, who also lived in Frederick, even wrote Whittier claiming that she, not Mrs. Frietchie, was the plucky woman who had waved the Union flag. "That there was a Dame Frietchie in Frederick who loved the flag is not disputed by anyone," said Whittier stoutly. "As for the rest I do not feel responsible. If there was no such occurrence, so much the worse for Frederick City."[50]

❀ Gaither, Rowan (1909–1961)

OVERALL-AIM-OF-FORD-FOUNDATION QUOTE "The overall aim of the Ford Foundation is to so alter life in the U.S. that we can be comfortably merged with the Soviet Union."

Radical rightists in the United States have been quoting the
aim-of-the-Ford-Foundation statement since the early 1950s,
sometimes attributing it to Rowan Gaither, president and
chairman of the Ford Foundation for many years, and sometimes to an unnamed source. At first they claimed Gaither
had uttered the words during Congressional hearings on tax-
exempt foundations in 1952, but when informed that the record of the proceedings contained no such statement, they
insisted that he said it in an aside during a break in the hearings. It is about as likely that Gaither said this as it is that
President Richard Nixon worked (as John Birchers charged)
to change the economic and political structure of the United
States so "it can be comfortably merged with Soviet Russia."[51]

❀ Galileo (1564–1642)

DOES-MOVE QUOTE   *"Eppur si muove"* (And yet it moves).

There is no evidence that Galileo stubbornly whispered these
defiant words after being forced by the Inquisition in 1633
to abjure his belief that the earth revolved around the sun.
It was a French writer, writing more than a century after
Galileo's death, who first put the words in the great scientist's mouth. But they surely represented Galileo's firm belief.[52]

❀ Garbo, Greta (1905–   )

GO-HOME QUOTE   "I t'ank I go home."

There are a couple of stories about the origin of this remark,
but it is doubtful that Garbo ever made it. One story has it
that while making her first American film, *The Torrent*
(1926), Garbo had to plunge into an icy pool of water for
one scene. She emerged, trembling with cold. "Fine," said

the director, "now let's do it again." Once more she plunged into the icy water and came out shivering and shaking. "That's it," beamed the director. "Now let's do it again." At that point Garbo is said to have picked up her coat and walked away saying, "I t'ank I go home." But another story relates that in 1927 Garbo put pressure on MGM head Louis B. Mayer for more money. "Greta," said Mayer, "haven't I done everything to make you happy here?" "No," said Garbo. "Give me more money." "Why?" cried Mayer. "You are paying Jack Gilbert ten thousand a week," said Garbo. "How much will make you happy?" asked Mayer. "Five thousand dollars a week," said Garbo. "I'll give you twenty-five hundred," Mayer told her. "I t'ank I go home," she said. Mayer then caved in and agreed to $5000. It's an unlikely story.[53]

❈ Garfield, James A. (1831–1881)

CHEAP-LABOR QUOTE—"I take it that . . . individuals or companies have the right to buy labor where they can get it cheaper. We have a treaty with the Chinese government which should be religiously kept . . . and I am not prepared to say that it should be abrogated until our great manufacturing and corporate interests are conserved in the matter of labor."

When James A. Garfield was running for President on the Republican ticket in 1880, a New York scandal sheet called *Truth* came out with a letter Garfield was said to have written H. L. Morey of the Employers Union in Lynn, Massachusetts, favoring the importation of cheap Chinese labor into the country. Soon the Democrats were distributing flyers publicizing the letter, and it began to look as though it would hurt Garfield with American labor, especially on the West Coast. But Garfield vehemently denied having ever expressed such sentiments, and before long the Republicans were able to prove the statement a fake. There was no such person as H. L. Morey, for one thing, and, for another, there was no Employers Union in Lynn or anywhere else. The Democrats apologized; and newspapers carried Garfield's denial alongside the cheap-labor statement. No one knows who faked the Morey letter, but it quickly died as a campaign issue. Garfield won the election in November.[54]

GOVERNMENT-STILL-LIVES QUOTE   "Fellow citizens! Clouds and darkness are found round Him! His pavilion is dark waters and thick clouds of the skies! Justice and judgment are the establishment of His throne! Mercy and truth shall go before His face! Fellow citizens! God reigns, and the Government at Washington still lives!"

When Garfield was running for President in 1880, his campaign biographers made much of a dramatic speech he was supposed to have given in April 1865, from which the above hyperventilated passage is taken. He was in New York City, they reported, when news of Abraham Lincoln's assassination arrived; and as he watched angry crowds gather in the streets and head for the offices of the anti-Lincoln *New York World*, he stepped forward, holding a small flag, lifted his right arm, and made the statement. Garfield's words, it was said, held the crowd spellbound. The people, according to campaign biographies, "stood riveted to the ground with awe, gazing at the motionless orator, and thinking of God and the security of the Government at that hour. . . . What might have happened had the surging and maddened crowd been let loose, none can tell. The man for the crisis was on the spot, more potent than Napoleon's guns at Paris." It's a splendid story, but unfortunately it's not true. Garfield, an Ohio Congressman at the time, wasn't even in New York in April 1865.[55]

❄ Gaulle, Charles de (1890–1970)

INEVITABLE-COMMUNISM QUOTE   "The evolution toward Communism is inevitable."

Some extreme rightists in the United States regarded France's General de Gaulle as soft on Communism, but conservative writer and editor William F. Buckley, Jr., was not one of them. In November 1962, Buckley's *National Review* warned its readers against a bit of "Gaullist Apocrypha" which had first appeared in France and was beginning to circulate in the United States. The document in question contained quotes from a purported conversation between French President de Gaulle and General de Beaufort in the spring of 1960. In the exchange, de Gaulle is supposed to have said that "the evolution toward Communism is inevitable," that he gave himself "two years after peace is established with Algeria to make France into a Communist country," and that "he has the strongest reasons to believe that [President John F.] Kennedy would accept a Communist Europe. . . ." Benjamin Potter, editor of the monthly bulletin, *Today in France,* first called the fake quotes to the attention of the *National Review,* and the editors were anxious to discredit them before they came to be regarded as authoritative "in the manner of a number of equally apocryphal statements attributed to Lenin, Stalin, Dimitrov, and Khrushchev."[56]

JOAN-OF-ARC QUOTE   "I am Joan of Arc. I am Clemenceau."

When Franklin Roosevelt and Charles de Gaulle met for the first time in Casablanca in January 1943, they took an instant dislike to each other. De Gaulle resented the fact that FDR did most of the talking and FDR thought de Gaulle was too sure of his position as leader of the Free French forces fighting the Nazis. After the meeting FDR told Secre-

tary of State Cordell Hull that the French General had
walked up to him and, insisting that he represented the
spirit of France, announced: "I am Joan of Arc. I am Clemenceau." To some of FDR's other associates the President
embroidered the story. "General," he said he told de Gaulle,
"you told me the other day you were Jeanne d'Arc and now
you say you are Clemenceau. Who are you?" "I am both,"
de Gaulle is supposed to have replied, and then, FDR said,
he told de Gaulle that "he should make up his mind which
one of these he was really like because he surely couldn't be
like both of them."

FDR's tale was soon circulating widely and steadily ex-
panding as it did so. By the time it got into American newspapers and magazines de Gaulle was alleged to have compared
himself to Louis XIV, Marshal Ferdinand Foch, Seigneur
de Bayard, Jean Baptiste, and other famous French figures,
as well as to Joan of Arc and Georges Clemenceau. But according to Harry Hopkins, FDR's chief aide at the Casablanca conference, the story was "pure fiction"; it was simply
FDR's way of conveying to his associates the kind of impression de Gaulle had made on him. When de Gaulle heard
about the FDR story he was highly incensed, and said he
"never wanted again to meet the President."[57]

❀ Gibbon, Edward (1737–1794)

RELIGIONS-EQUALLY-TRUE-AND-FALSE QUOTE "All religions
seem to the people equally true, to the philosopher equally
false, and to the magistrate equally useful."

Historian Gibbon was an agnostic and took what C. W. Wedgwood calls an attitude of "ironical superiority" toward believers, but the much-quoted statement about religions from
The Decline and Fall of the Roman Empire actually reads:
"The various modes of worship which prevailed in the Ro-

man world were all considered by the people equally true, by the philosophers equally false, and by the magistrates equally useful." He was reporting, not expressing an opinion, in the passage.[58]

❄ Gipp, George (1895–1920)

THE WIN-ONE QUOTE   "Win one for the Gipper!"

The Gipper quote was one of President Reagan's favorites. He not only inserted it into speeches; he also enjoyed explaining its origin. George Gipp, fabulous Notre Dame football player, Reagan liked to remind people, died young; he was only a college senior when he passed away in 1920. But just before expiring he supposedly told head coach Knute Rockne, "Win one for the Gipper!" Eight years later, during Notre Dame's worst season, Rockne finally decided to use Gipp's dying words to spur his team onward in its battle with Army. It worked; after Rockne used the Gipper quote at halftime, his team went on to move the score from 0–0 at the half to 12–6 at the end.

Reagan, a one-time sports announcer, had long known about the Gipper quote and had used it on his radio show in the early 1930s. And after going into movies and hearing that Warner Brothers planned to film *Knute Rockne—All American* (1940), he eagerly sought the part of George Gipp. To his delight he won the part and got to utter the immortal line in the film. His pal Pat O'Brien played Rockne in the football biopic.

Did George Gipp actually utter the deathbed plea? Probably not. Rockne was in the habit of thinking up all kinds of dramatic tales to inspire his players, and the Gipp story was almost certainly one of them. Reagan himself admitted that Rockne may have invented the tale, but he didn't think it mattered, because it inspired his team "to sacrifice their individual quarrels for a common goal." When Reagan spoke at the Notre Dame commencement in the spring of 1981, with Pat O'Brien on the platform by his side, he made the Gipper plea the center of his remarks. "Rockne could have used Gipp's dying words to win a game at any time," he told his audience. "But eight years went by following the death of George Gipp before Rockne revealed those dying words. . . . And then he told the story at halftime to a team that was losing and one of the only teams he had ever coached that was torn by dissension and jealousy and factionalism. . . . It was to this team that Rockne told the story and so inspired them that they rose above their personal animosities. For someone they had never known they joined together in a common cause and attained the unattainable."[59]

❀ Goering, Hermann (1893–1946)

REACH-FOR-REVOLVER QUOTE   "Whenever I hear the word culture, I reach for my revolver."

This statement is barbarous enough to sound like Nazi Reich Marshal Hermann Goering, but it actually comes from Hanns Johst's drama *Schlageter,* produced at the State Playhouse in Berlin in 1933, the year Adolf Hitler came to power in Germany. A *New York Times* reporter covering the play on May 28, 1933, summed up the play's message: "If you don't believe that everything worthwhile in history has been won by slaughter . . . you won't go home happy."[60]

❀ Goldwater, Barry M. (1909–   )

FRATERNITIES QUOTE   "Where fraternities are not allowed, communism flourishes."

In the early 1960s, Arizona's conservative Republican Senator Barry M. Goldwater remarked, just before making a speech to some college students in Los Angeles, that he couldn't understand why so many Harvard students accepted the Keynesian economic philosophy; later on, he said something about the value of college fraternities. The *Baltimore Catholic Review* thereupon quoted him as saying that at colleges where there are no fraternities, communism flourishes. Challenged as to the accuracy of the quote, the wire service which circulated the story explained that the reporter had confused "Keynesianism" with Communism.[61]

❀ Goldwyn, Sam (1882–1974)

BLANKET-CHECK QUOTE   "Look, Orson, if you'll just say yes to doing a picture with me, I'll give you a blanket check right now."

For years Hollywood movie producer Sam Goldwyn kept after Orson Welles to make a film for him. Once, close to midnight, he backed Welles into a corner and argued so forcibly that the great film-maker seemed to be yielding. Finally Goldwyn cried: "Look, Orson, if you'll just say yes to doing a picture with me, I'll give you a blank check right now." But a gossip columnist reported that Goldwyn had said, "blanket check." The report angered Goldwyn. He was even angrier when the *Reader's Digest* printed the blanket-check quote in its "Picturesque Patter of Speech" column and sent him a check for $25.[62]

BLOOD-AND-THIRSTY QUOTE   "I am very sorry that you felt it was too blood and thirsty."

After Goldwyn produced *The Secret Life of Walter Mitty* (1947), a film based on a James Thurber story in the *New*

Yorker about a Caspar Milquetoast who is courageous only in fantasy, he heard that Thurber was displeased with the film because the dream sequences had too much gore and violence in them for his gentle little tale. There's a story that Goldwyn wrote Thurber: "I am very sorry that you felt it was too blood and thirsty." Whereupon Thurber is said to have wired back: "Not only did I think so, but I was horror and struck." But this delightful exchange never took place. Goldwyn's secretaries, who prepared the letters he dictated, would have seen to that.[63]

BRINK-OF-ABSCESS QUOTE   "I was on the brink of a great abscess."

Once, when Goldwyn was ill, he was quoted as making this remark to friends, but, as with so many other Goldwynisms, it was just another invention of someone on his staff. Goldwyn knew the difference between abyss and abscess.[64]

BULL-BY-TEETH QUOTE   "You've got to take the bull by the teeth."

This is another popular—but fake—Goldwynism.[65]

CAUSTIC QUOTE   "To hell with the cost. If it's a good story, I'll make it."

One day Goldwyn's associates at the studio came to him to warn against a certain property because "it's too caustic for films." "To hell with the cost," Goldwyn is supposed to have exclaimed. "If it's a good story, I'll make it." But Arthur Marx, Goldwyn's biographer, relegated this story to the large body of Goldwyn apocrypha and thought it was coined either by a gag man for a Goldwyn picture or by a press agent.[66]

COMEDIES-NOT-TO-BE-LAUGHED-AT QUOTE   "Our comedies are not to be laughed at."

Journalist Alva Johnston, who wrote a great deal about movies during Hollywood's Golden Era, maintained that this line came not from Goldwyn but was an old Hollywood quip.[67]

DUCK QUOTE   "It rolls off my back like a duck."

George Oppenheimer, theater critic for *Newsday*, once revealed that he had made up many spurious Goldwynisms when he was a scriptwriter in Hollywood. " 'It rolls off my back like a duck' was one of mine," he declared. "I remember springing it for the first time on Dotty Parker and Edna Ferber when we were all sitting around the writers' table in the commissary one day." Oppenheimer won the prize that day (each writer had contributed $10 to the pot) for the best Goldwyn gaffe the diners could think up.[68]

FLASHLIGHT QUOTE   "Quick as a flashlight!"

Irving Fein, Goldwyn's assistant publicity director in the 1940s, once said: "Sure, we used to make up Goldwynisms all the time in order to get publicity breaks. I remember one right now that I made up—'Quick as a flashlight.' "[69]

HAIR-STAND-ON-EDGE-OF-SEAT QUOTE   "When I see the pictures you play in that theater it makes the hair stand on the edge of my seat."

Goldwyn made this remark, according to legend, to the manager of New York City's Rialto Theater, which specialized in horror films and instructed the telephone operator to answer calls from patrons with the words, "Help, murder, police! This is the Rialto, now playing . . . ." But Goldwyn didn't make the remark. It was Hungarian director Michael Curtiz, a marvelous mangler of the language himself, who came out with the remark in a chat with MGM mogul Louis B. Mayer.[70]

IM-POSSIBLE QUOTE   "I can answer you in two words—impossible!"

According to *Saturday Evening Post* writer Alva Johnston, this line first appeared in a humor magazine late in 1925, and was later assigned to Goldwyn.[71]

INCLUDE-ME-OUT QUOTE   "Gentlemen, include me out!"

Most Goldwyn aficionados believe that the famous moviemaker uttered his most famous line at a meeting of the Motion Picture Producers and Distributors of America, which had been called to discuss labor difficulties with a Hollywood union head named Willie Bioff. During the meeting, they say, when Goldwyn disagreed with one of the decisions his associates made, he got up, reached for his hat, and cried: "Gentlemen, include me out!" But Goldwyn always denied he had said anything like that. What he said, he insisted, was: "Gentlemen, I'm withdrawing from the association."

Goldwyn blamed playwright George S. Kaufman and comedian Eddie Cantor, as well as overzealous press agents, for many of the tongue-slips attributed to him. But he also admitted that he really did commit a few gaffes on his own. "Chances are that in my lifetime I have said a few things not according to Hoyle," he said toward the end of his life. "After all, I'm not a graduate of Oxford or high school or even grammar school. . . . I've made errors in speech, but so have scholars."[72]

INDIANS QUOTE   "We can get all the Indians we need at the reservoir."

No one knows what film-maker (if any) made this remark, when assembling the cast for a Western movie, but it was not Goldwyn.[73]

MAKE-THEM-AMERICANS QUOTE   "Don't worry about that. We'll make them Americans."

When Lillian Hellman's play, *The Children's Hour,* opened to glowing reviews on Broadway in 1934, Sam Goldwyn told associate producer Merritt Hulburd, "Maybe we ought to buy it." "Forget it, Mr. Goldwyn," Hulburd is supposed to have said. "It's about lesbians." "Don't worry about that," Goldwyn is said to have responded. "We'll make them Americans."

The quote is apocryphal. Goldwyn was too sophisticated to have said anything so silly. He had Hellman under contract as a screenwriter, moreover, long before he ever thought of filming her play, and since he frequently had lunch with her, it is extremely likely that they discussed her hit play at some point.[74]

MUCUS QUOTE   "First you have a good story, then a good treatment, and next a first-rate director. After that you hire a competent cast, and even then you have only the mucus of a good picture."

What Goldwyn actually said was, "even then you have only the nucleus of a good picture." But reporters picked up his statement, substituted "mucus" for "nucleus," and made the revised version famous.

At first Goldwyn seems not to have minded the apocrypha that clustered around him, for they helped win attention for his films. But his desire to be known as a film-maker of quality made him increasingly irked by the malapropisms committed in his name. "None of them are true," he finally declared. "They're all made up by a bunch of comedians and pinned on me."[75]

NEXT-TIME-I-SEND-A-FOOL QUOTE   "The next time I send a damn fool for something, I go myself."

It was the tongue-twisting Hungarian director Michael Curtiz, not Goldwyn, who made this priceless remark. He lost his temper when a messenger whom he had sent off to get a prop for a scene he was filming came back with the wrong thing.[76]

READ-PART-OF-IT QUOTE   "I read part of it all the way through."

Goldwyn could have said this—so could several other producers—but he never did.[77]

PSYCHIATRIST QUOTE   "Anyone who would go to a psychiatrist ought to have his head examined."

No one knows who first made this remark, but it was not Goldwyn. Someone on his staff seems to have put it into circulation.[78]

S.O.B. QUOTE   "Never let that sonofabitch in this office again—unless we need him."

There is no evidence that Goldwyn ever made this statement. It was an old Hollywood remark and first attached itself to MGM's Louis B. Mayer and then to Columbia Pictures's Harry Cohn. Then, when Goldwyn became well-known, it was attributed to him.[79]

VERBAL-CONTRACT QUOTE   "A verbal contract isn't worth the paper it's written on."

What Goldwyn really said of movie executive Joseph M. Schenck (whom people regarded as absolutely trustworthy) was: "His verbal contract is worth more than the paper it's written on." But the manufacturers of Goldwyn gems quickly changed this to, "a verbal contract isn't worth the paper it's written on," and sent it out to the world.[80]

❀ Gordon, Sol (1923–)

ANTI-MARRIAGE QUOTE "All that is good and commendable now existing would continue to exist if all marriage laws were repealed tomorrow. I have an inalienable constitutional and natural right to love whom I may . . . [and] to change that love every day if I please."

In 1980 the Council for National Righteousness distributed a pamphlet entitled *The Unbelievable Truth about Public Schools,* printed in Buffalo, New York, in which it quoted Sol Gordon, author of *Facts about Sex for Today's Youth,* as having made the above statement advocating free love. But the statement does not appear anywhere in Gordon's book; nor did he ever put the words in any of his other publications. One of his books, indeed, is entitled, *Raising a Child Conservatively in a Sexually Permissive World* (New York, 1983). Gordon complained that his critics were wont to quote him out of context, but "now they blatantly compose their own statements."[81]

❀ Greeley, Horace (1811–1872)

GO-WEST QUOTE "Go west, young man. . . ."

In an article for Indiana's *Terre Haute Express* in 1851, John Babsone Soule (or Soulé) first gave this advice, and Greeley who reprinted the article in his *New York Tribune* saw to it that Soule got full credit. But nevertheless it didn't work out that way; ever afterwards the statement was attributed to Greeley.[82]

❀   Hall, Gus (1910–   )

STRANGLED-TO-DEATH QUOTE   "I dream of the hour when the
last Congressman is strangled to death on the guts of the last
preacher—and since Christians like to sing about the blood,
why not give them a little of it? Slit the throats of their children and drag them over the mourners' bench and the pulpit, and allow them to drown in their own blood, and then
see whether they enjoy singing these hymns."

When Gus Hall, General Secretary of the American Communist Party, was invited to speak at the University of Oregon
in 1962, there was an outburst of protest in Eugene, where
the university is located, and an outpouring of anti-Hall
posters and leaflets featuring the strangled-to-death statement
which Hall was charged with having made at a Communist convention in 1937 and again at the funeral of Communist leader Eugene Dennis in 1961. But the *New York
Times*, which covered the Dennis funeral, mentioned no
such bloodcurdling statement in Hall's eulogy, and Hall himself, when queried about it by reporters in Eugene, said the
statement was so vile he wouldn't bother denying it. The
attribution of the inflammatory words to Hall first appeared
in reactionary Kenneth Goff's *Pilgrim Torch* in April 1961,
but actually they can be traced back to Jean Meslier (a
Catholic who turned anti-Christian), whose will, published
by Voltaire in 1733, stated: "I should like to see . . . the
last king strangled with the guts of the last priest." In 1980,
evangelist Jerry Falwell's Moral Majority used the phony
Gus Hall quotation in a multi-media presentation entitled,
"America, You're Too Young to Die."[88]

❀   Hecht, Ben (1893–1964)

EXECUTING-CHRIST QUOTE   "One of the finest things ever done
by the mob was the crucifixion of Christ. Intellectually it was

a splendid gesture. But trust the mob to bungle. If I had charge of executing Christ, I would have handled it differently. You see what I would have done was had him shipped to Rome and fed to the lions. They never could have made a savior out of mince meat."

In March 1964, Elizabeth Shepherd issued a leaflet called, "Who Are the Haters?," which contained writer Ben Hecht's executing-Christians quote. The quote was picked up by anti-Semitic groups around the country and even used by some ultra-conservative groups which were not anti-Semitic. But there is irony in the use—or, rather, misuse—of this particular quote. The passage appears in Hecht's novel, *A Jew in Love* (1931), but it is uttered by an anti-Communist named Boshere. And Boshere, after making his remark about feeding Christians to the lions, adds: "I would do the same thing to radicals today."[84]

❀ Hitler, Adolf (1889–1945)

LAW-AND-ORDER QUOTE   "The streets of our country are in turmoil. The universities are filled with students rebelling and rioting. Communists are seeking to destroy our country. Russia is threatening us with her might and the Republic is in danger. Yes, danger from within and without. We need law and order! Yes, without law and order our nation cannot survive. . . . Elect us and we shall restore law and order. We shall, by law and order, be respected among the nations of the world. Without law and order our Republic shall fall."

The law-and-order statement, supposedly made by Nazi dictator Hitler in a campaign speech in Hamburg in 1932, the year before he came into power, is a kiss-of-death quote. Since its source is so disreputable, it has been used to discredit proponents of law and order, who, the Hitler-quoters suggest, have Nazi sympathies. During the Stormy Sixties,

antiwar protests on American college campuses became so
unruly at times that there were calls for a crackdown on student activities; and critics of the Vietnam War, like Democratic Senator Edmund Muskie of Maine and U.S. Supreme
Court Justice William O. Douglas, who sympathized with
student dissidents, both used the Hitler quote to warn against
the threat of repressive measures to civil liberties in the
United States.

But the Hitler quote is an obvious fake. The only students
who were rebelling and rioting in Germany in 1932, as philosopher Sidney Hook has pointed out, were Nazi students
protesting against the presence of Jewish professors on university faculties. And the candidate for law and order in Germany in 1932 was not Hitler, but Field Marshal Paul von
Hindenberg. Hitler was calling for a Nazi revolution, not for
law and order.

The Hitler quote originally appeared in an obscure Communist periodical, began turning up on posters on American
college campuses in the late sixties, was featured by anti-
Vietnam demonstrators during the 1968 presidential campaign, and was even used in *Billy Jack* (1971), a movie about
a "freedom school" composed of racially mixed students who
were being persecuted by vicious bigots in the neighboring
town.

Both Senator Muskie and Justice Douglas apologized for
using the quote after learning it was a fake, and the latter
removed it from the next printing of his book, *Points of
Rebellion* (1970). But the quote continued to be popular
in some leftist circles.[85]

❀   Holmes, Oliver Wendell, Jr. (1841–1935)

KEEP-GOVERNMENT-POOR QUOTE   "Keep government poor and
remain free."

In a speech on June 15, 1982, President Ronald Reagan quoted Justice Holmes as having advised the American people to "keep government poor and remain free." But a White House official admitted that the President "came up with that one himself. Holmes never said anything point-blank exactly like that. . . . We're still trying to track it down." Holmes scholar Ed Bander of the Suffolk Law School in Boston doubted they would ever be able to locate any such statement in Holmes's writings.[86]

❀ Holmes, Sherlock

ELEMENTARY-WATSON QUOTE "Elementary, my dear Watson."

Between 1887 and 1927 British writer A. Conan Doyle published four novels and fifty-six short stories about the celebrated detective Sherlock Holmes and his physician-friend Dr. John H. Watson. But not even once did he have Holmes utter the well-known phrase. It was Basil Rathbone, British actor playing the ratiocinative sleuth in a series of Hollywood movies appearing in the 1930s and 1940s, who made the words famous.[87]

❀ Hoover, Herbert (1874–1964)

NOBLE-EXPERIMENT QUOTE Prohibition is "a noble experiment."

To the end of his life Herbert Hoover denied he had ever called the Eighteenth (Prohibition) Amendment (1919) a "noble experiment." What he had said was that Prohibition was "a great social and economic experiment, noble in motive." But the noble-experiment quote was popular with foes of Prohibition, who insisted Hoover had made a fatuous remark about it. Some observers doubted that it misrepresented his views, but Hoover thought it did.[88]

PROSPERITY-AROUND-THE-CORNER QUOTE   "Prosperity is just around the corner."

When the Great Depression hit the United States after the stock market collapse in the fall of 1929, President Hoover made periodic statements assuring the American people that the economy would eventually right itself, but he never did say prosperity was "just around the corner." In an address at the annual dinner of the Chamber of Commerce of the United States in 1931, however, he did announce that "we have now passed the worst and with continued unity of effort we shall rapidly recover. There is one certainty of the future of a people of the resources, intelligence, and character of the people of the United States—that is, prosperity."[89]

❀   Hopkins, Harry (1890–1946)

DAMN-DUMB QUOTE   "The people are too damn dumb to understand."

Opponents of the New Deal and the welfare state have gotten a lot of mileage out of a remark New Dealer Harry Hopkins is supposed to have made that revealed his contempt for the American people. But the Hopkins quote is spurious. It originated in a press conference which Hopkins gave when he was administering Civil Works Administration relief projects in the early 1930s. One of these projects involved a study of ancient safety pins, and at the press conference one of the reporters made a facetious reference to the project and asked if Hopkins was going to make an investigation of projects like that in New York. "Why should I?" exclaimed Hopkins testily. "There is nothing the matter with that. They are damn good projects—excellent projects. That goes for all the projects up there. You know some people make fun of people who speak a foreign language, and dumb people criticize something they do not understand, and that is what is going on up there—God damn it! Here are a lot of people broke and we are putting them to work making researches of one kind or another. . . . We have projects up there to make Jewish dictionaries. There are rabbis who are broke and on the relief rolls. One hundred and fifty projects up there deal with pure science. What of it? I think those things are good in life. . . ."

But reports of the Hopkins press conference quoted the CWA director as having said the American people were "too damn dumb" and many scathing editorials were written denouncing Hopkins and all New Dealers. The *Washington Post* even published a poem by a Virginia lady containing this verse:

> Though we still pay our tax,
>   Mr. Hopkins!
> We are sharpening the ax,
>   Mr. Hopkins!
> Testing it with cautious thumb—
> And we're telling you, by gum,
> We are not quite too damn dumb,
>   Mr. Hopkins![90]

TAX-SPEND-ELECT QUOTE "Tax and tax, spend and spend, elect and elect."

For years American conservatives have quoted the tax-spend-elect statement to show how cynical New Dealers were when they sponsored public-works programs in the 1930s and how unashamedly their liberal successors in Congress and the White House have followed in their footsteps ever since. The remark, they say, was made by Harry Hopkins (formerly CWA head) when he headed the Works Progress Administration (WPA), a New Deal agency which spent billions in the 1930s to provide jobs for the unemployed during the Great Depression.

But Hopkins never made the remark. "He didn't have to," declared Sherwin D. Smith in an article about WPA for the *New York Times* in 1965. FDR's Vice-President, John Nance Garner, Smith noted, said it all when Congress passed the first WPA appropriation in 1933: "You can't beat $4,880,000,000." But that was Garner, not Hopkins. Hopkins himself tried hard to keep politics out of WPA. "I thought at first I could be completely non-political," he once declared. "Then they told me I had to be part non-political and part political. I found that was impossible, at least for me. I finally realized there was nothing for it but to be all-political." Still, he strove to be non-partisan. He appointed so many Republicans to powerful WPA administrative posts that the Democrats began complaining about it. He also issued strict instructions: WPA workers weren't to be pressured by politicians, or forced to support any political party or candidate, financially or otherwise, or told how to vote. Yet because WPA workers, grateful for their jobs, inevitably voted Democratic, Hopkins was accused of playing politics.

It was Frank R. Kent, conservative newspaper columnist, who first put the tax-spend-elect remark in print. But when Hopkins heard about it, he categorically denied ever having made such a remark. "I deny the whole works and the whole implication of it," he announced. But, like the damn-dumb quote, it came to be accepted as authentic; and when the Senate Commerce Committee held hearings on Hopkins's appointment as Secretary of Commerce in 1938, there were many questions about the statement. In the end, though, the Senate confirmed the appointment.

Kent reported the tax-spend-elect remark but he didn't originate it. It was Max Gordon, New York theatrical producer, who first put the words in Hopkins's mouth. One day he met Hopkins at the Empire City Race Track, along with Heywood Broun, liberal columnist, and Daniel Arnstein,

New York transportation specialist. The four men talked about many things that afternoon, but afterwards Gordon quoted Hopkins on taxing, spending, and electing, and the remark quickly made its way into Frank Kent's column. But when Broun and Arnstein were asked about it, neither could recall such a remark at the racetrack. And Gordon himself later admitted that Hopkins hadn't actually used those precise words; but, he insisted, "That's what he meant!" Or, one supposes, what Gordon thought he meant.

In the 1980s the Hopkins quote reappeared in a revised form to make fun of the Reagan administration's massive deficit-financing policies: "Borrow and borrow, spend and spend."[91]

✿ Howard, Roy (1883–1964)

TOO-MUCH-CHECKING-FACTS QUOTE   "Too much checking on the facts has ruined many a good news story."

In June 1985, Chief Justice Warren Burger quoted Roy Howard, head of the Scripps-Howard newspaper chain for decades, as having made this cynical remark, but there is no evidence that he ever did. His former associates strongly doubted he said anything of the kind, and diligent research in the Roy Howard papers at the Roy Howard Memorial Center at the Indiana University School of Journalism has failed to locate such a statement.[92]

✿ Humanist Manifesto II (1973)

UNBRIDLED-SEXUALITY QUOTE   "There should be no restraint on any expression of human sexuality. Unbridled sexuality is not immoral. In fact it is healthful and good."

In the fall of 1981, evangelist Pat Robertson's magazine, *Pat Robertson's Perspective,* charged that secular humanists encouraged sexual promiscuity, and quoted the above statement from a pronouncement by some prominent humanists to back up its charge. But the Humanist Manifesto, issued in 1973, forty years after Humanist Manifesto I, contained no such statement. In one place, in fact, the Manifesto appearing in *The Humanist,* organ of the American Humanist Association, declared: "Without countenancing mindless permissiveness or unbridled promiscuity, a civilized society should be a *tolerant* one."[93]

✿ Ickes, Harold (1874–1952)

MODIFIED-COMMUNISM QUOTE   "What we were striving for was a kind of modified form of communism."

In December 1981, President Ronald Reagan remarked that Harold Ickes, Franklin Roosevelt's Secretary of Interior and an ardent New Dealer, had made this statement "in his book," presumably meaning his diary, which was published in three volumes after his death. But there is no such statement in the Ickes diaries; and a White House spokeswoman, queried by reporters, was unable to clarify the President's reference. There was nothing in Ickes's writings, in fact, that supported either fascism or communism.[94]

✿ Ingersoll, Robert G. (1833–1899)

HUMBLEST-PEASANT QUOTE   "I would rather be the humblest peasant that ever lived . . . at peace with the world than be the greatest Christian that ever lived."

In a speech attacking Robert Ingersoll, the "Great Agnostic," on May 26, 1912, evangelist Billy Sunday put these words in Ingersoll's mouth, and they have been quoted ever since. But Ingersoll never said them. What he did say, in his famous soliloquy at the tomb of Napoleon in 1882, was that he "would rather have been a French peasant and worn wooden shoes . . . than to have been that imperial impersonation of force and murder known as Napoleon the Great."[95]

❄ Jackson, Andrew (1767–1845)

LET-HIM-ENFORCE-IT QUOTE "John Marshall has made his decision. Now let him enforce it!"

When a Georgia law, passed in 1830, ordered white residents in the Cherokee country to take an oath of allegiance to the state, two New England missionaries refused to do so and were arrested. They then took their case to the federal courts, and in 1832 Chief Justice John Marshall handed down a Supreme Court ruling (*Worcester v. Georgia*) that the national government held exclusive jurisdiction over the territory of the Cherokee Nation and that the Georgia law was unconstitutional. But President Jackson, who sympathized with Georgia, is supposed to have exclaimed after hearing of the Marshall decision: "Well: John Marshall has made his decision; *now let him enforce it!*" The statement sounds like Jackson, but he didn't make it, according to historian Robbert V. Remini, though he certainly felt that way about the decision. "The decision of the supreme court has fell still born," he wrote John Coffee, "and they find that it cannot coerce Georgia to yield to its mandate." The missionaries were released from prison in 1833.[96]

ONE-MAN-WITH-COURAGE QUOTE "One man with courage makes a majority."

On October 10, 1987, when his nomination of Judge Robert Bork to the U.S. Supreme Court ran into trouble in the U.S. Senate, President Reagan announced: "Andrew Jackson once said that one man with courage makes a majority. Obviously, Bob Bork has that courage." But Rena G. Kunis, writing in the *New York Times* shortly afterwards, was unable to locate the remark in Jackson's writings.

Kunis noted that John Knox, 16th-century Protestant reformer, had said: "A man with God is always in the majority," that abolitionist Wendell Phillips had said, "One on God's side is a majority," and that Henry David Thoreau had said, "Any man more right than his neighbors constitutes a majority of one." Jackson certainly behaved at times as if he agreed with these sentiments, but there is no record of his having made a similar statement.[97]

VICTORS-SPOILS QUOTE   "To the victors belong the spoils."

Though sometimes attributed to Jackson, the victor-spoils remark was not his but New York Senator William L. Marcy's. In January 1832, when Jackson nominated Martin Van Buren as minister to Britain, Henry Clay denounced the latter for bringing patronage practices he had developed in Albany into national politics, and Marcy strongly defended Van Buren, his fellow New Yorker. "It may be, sir," he told Clay, "that the politicians of the United States are not so fastidious as some gentlemen are, as to disclosing the principles on which they act. They boldly practice what they preach. When they are contending for victory, they avow their intention of enjoying the fruits of it. If they are defeated, they expect to retire from office. They see nothing wrong in the rule, that to the victor belong the spoils of the enemy."[98]

✿ Japanese Government Memo (1987)

COMPETING-FOR-JAPANESE-INVESTMENTS   QUOTE   "We   now
have various states in the U.S. competing against each other
for Japanese R & D and investments. Whatever administration is in power, we can now virtually defy the U.S. on a
number of trade issues, and have many governors and Congressmen assisting us in the process."

On May 30, 1987, Democratic Congressman Tom McMillen
of Maryland took to the floor of the House of Representatives
to quote from the translation of an "internal, high-level
Japanese Government memo" which stated that Japanese
investments in the United States would be targeted to Congressional districts where they would do the most good for
Japan. The document, according to McMillen, urged Japan's
Prime Minister to "coordinate Japanese investment strategies
in the U.S. to maximize the political pay-offs vis-à-vis individual Congressional districts. Of course, Japanese interests
can still rely on the service of Washington lobbyists and
sympathetic former U.S. public officials to gain access when
needed. Still, we should have Japanese coordinating our interests."

When McMillen's colleagues in the House raised questions about the document and he took a closer look at it, he
discovered it was bogus. He had received his copy at a Congressional breakfast at which Ronald A. Morse, secretary of
the Asian program at the Woodrow Wilson Center for
Scholars, had distributed it during a discussion of U.S.-
Japan economic relations. Morse told the law-makers he had
written the document himself to dramatize Japanese attitudes
toward investment in the United States, but apparently he
hadn't made it exactly clear what he was doing. "I don't
recall his saying it was bogus," complained one of McMillen's colleagues. "The guy at the Wilson Center didn't explain it real well," grumbled a foreign-investment specialist

on McMillen's staff. Whether the bogus Japanese-investment quote would pass into general circulation remained an open question.[99]

❁ Jefferson, Thomas (1743–1826)

BEST-GOVERNMENT QUOTE   "That government is best which governs least."

In his nationally syndicated column for November 11, 1987, William F. Buckley, Jr., urged Republicans to remember "the insight of the earliest Democratic President. It was Thomas Jefferson who said that the government is best which governs least. . . ." Buckley was quoting one of the most popular Jefferson sayings in circulation, but the Sage of Monticello did not, in fact, ever make the remark. It appears in the first sentence of Henry David Thoreau's famous essay on civil disobedience, first published in 1849, but it is not Thoreau's statement either, for he put quotation marks around it, as if it were an old saying.[100]

ETERNAL-VIGILANCE QUOTE   "Eternal vigilance is the price of liberty."

Though often attributed to Jefferson, the much-cited eternal-vigilance statement appears nowhere in Jefferson's writings. Nor, for that matter, does it appear in the writings of any other famous American. And for that, in the opinion of Seattle writer Kenneth L. Calkins, "we can be thankful. Self-proclaimed patriots of many lands have used the quotation as justification for suspension of civil liberties."[101]

❀ Jones, John Paul (1747–1792)

NOT-YET-BEGUN-TO-FIGHT QUOTE "I have not yet begun to fight."

When John Paul Jones's *Bonhomme Richard* engaged the British warship *Serapis* in battle on September 23, 1779, did the doughty commander actually exclaim, "I have not yet begun to fight," when the British called on him to surrender? He might have, but there is no evidence that he did. In his own account of the battle afterward, he didn't mention the dramatic words, and he probably would have had he uttered them.[102]

❀ Kant, Immanuel (1724–1804)

COPERNICAN-REVOLUTION QUOTE Kant called his critical philosophy a "Copernican revolution."

For years, eminent scholars, among them Bertrand Russell, John Dewey, and Karl Popper, have believed that the great German philosopher announced he had effected a "Copernican revolution" in metaphysics by insisting that the objects of human knowledge are not "things-in-themselves," but products of an interaction between the mind and the external world. But Kant never made the statement. In the preface to the second edition of the *Critique of Pure Reason* (1787), he explained that his thinking proceeded "precisely on the lines of Copernicus's first thoughts *(mit den ersten Gedanken des Kopernikus)* "; and though he referred to Copernicus elsewhere in his writings he never spoke of a "Copernican revolution." Bertrand Russell, in fact, thought the Kantian philosophy could be called Ptolemaic, not Copernican, since Kant "put Man back at the centre from which Copernicus had dethroned him." But there is what might be called a

"Ptolemaic tendency" in all human beings, including scientists; we tend to think the universe is what we say it is.[103]

❀ Kautsky, Karl (1854–1938)

SOCIALIST-WORK QUOTE "Socialist production is not compatible with liberty of work, that is to say, with the worker's freedom to work when or how he likes. . . . It is true that under the rule of capitalism, a worker still enjoys liberty up to a certain degree. If he does not quite like a factory, he can find work elsewhere. In a socialist society, all the means of production will be concentrated in the hands of the state, and the latter will be the only employer; there will be no *choice*. The workman today *enjoys more liberty than he will possess in a socialist society.*"

In the introduction to an edition of the *Communist Manifesto* published in 1954, Stefan A. Possony stated that Karl Kautsky (one of the leading theoreticians of the German Social Democratic movement and a bitter opponent of Lenin) advocated "slave labor" under socialism; and, to prove his point, Possony cited the above passage, taken, he said, from one of Kautsky's major theoretical works, *Grundsaetzen und Foerderungen der Sozialdemokratie* (1892). But the Kautsky quote is a concoction. Not only is it completely out of harmony with the actual objectives of 19th-century socialist parties; key sentences have also been left out of the original Kautsky text, giving the passage a totally different meaning from what Kautsky had intended. The final sentence, the one in italics, doesn't even appear in the original. It was manufactured and tacked onto the misleading Kautsky quote.[104]

❀ Khrushchev, Nikita (1894–1971)

DOSES-OF-SOCIALISM QUOTE "We cannot expect the Americans to jump from capitalism to communism, but we can aid their elected leaders in giving them small doses of socialism until they suddenly awake to find they have communism."

Khrushchev's doses-of-socialism statement, supposedly made at a secret meeting in Moscow just before the Soviet leader visited the United States in 1959, turned up in the United States in 1960 and was soon being publicized by John Birchers and other ultra-conservatives. But researchers in the Library of Congress and the Central Intelligence Agency were unable to establish the authenticity of the quotation, and it turned out that it was the deliberate fabrication of some radical rightists in this country, who thought it summed up Khrushchev's attitude. Discussing the hoax in Congress, Montana Senator Lee Metcalf pointed out that "whoever created this quotation, and those who, knowing it to be spurious, nevertheless disseminate it, are cut from the same cloth as Communists and Fascists."[105]

GULLIBLE QUOTE "You Americans are so gullible. No, you won't accept Communism outright, but we'll keep feeding you small doses of Socialism until you'll finally wake up and find you already have Communism. We won't have to fight you. We'll so weaken your economy until you'll fall like an overripe fruit into our hands."

In the 1960s the doses-of-socialism quote merged with the Lenin overripe-fruit quote (see Lenin) to produce a real sizzler for extreme rightists to make gleeful use of in their publications. In 1969 former Secretary of Agriculture Ezra Taft Benson even recalled hearing Khrushchev recite these lines when the latter was visiting the country in 1959 when Dwight D. Eisenhower was President. Khrushchev was talkative when he was in the United States, and, as a devout

Marxist-Leninist, he made no secret of his belief that socialism was the wave of the future. But it strains credulity to
believe that he used the doses-of-socialism phrase (not fabricated until 1960), or even the overripe-fruit fake (which had
been circulating in the United States, not the Soviet Union,
since 1954), or that his interpreter chose those words when
translating his remarks. Benson may have heard what he
wanted to hear.[106]

TOO-LIBERAL-TO-FIGHT QUOTE   "American liberals are too liberal to fight."

In an interview in New York in September 1962, after returning from a ten-day visit to Russia, poet Robert Frost told
reporters that "Khrushchev said American liberals were too
liberal to fight." Frost's statement was quoted jubilantly by
John A. Stormer in *None Dare Call It Treason* (1964) and
by other right-wingers in speeches and publications. But
there is reason to believe that Frost's statement wasn't entirely accurate. When queried about the statement by Norman Thomas, Frost wrote the socialist leader (in a letter he
never got around to mailing before his death) as follows: "I
can't see how Khrushchev's talk got turned into what you
quote that we weren't man enough to fight. I came nearer
than he to threatening; with my native gentility I assured
him that we were no more afraid of him than he was of us."
He also said that during the conversation Khrushchev quoted
"either Gorky to Tolstoi or Tolstoi to Gorky, I forget which,
when he said there was such a thing possibly as a nation getting like the bald-headed row at a leg show so it enjoyed
wanting to do what it could no longer do." Applying this to
nations, Khrushchev insisted the United States was old and
the Soviet Union young. Frost apparently transformed this
comment into a remark about liberals.[107]

TREATIES-WITH-IMPERIALISTS QUOTE   "You should not take
too seriously the treaties made with the imperialists. Lenin,

too, signed a peace treaty after World War I that remained valid only so long as it proved necessary."

A pamphlet published by an extreme-rightist group, the Minutemen, entitled, *Principles of Guerrilla Warfare*, reported that Khrushchev made this statement at the Leipzig Fair in Germany in March 1959, but there is no record of his having done so. But the quote continued to circulate in this country long after Khrushchev was removed from office in 1964.[108]

❀ Kissinger, Henry (1923–   )

DAY-OF-UNITED-STATES-PAST QUOTE   "The day of the United States is past, and today is the day of the Soviet Union. . . . My job as Secretary of State is to negotiate the most acceptable second-best position available."

In a television speech in the spring of 1976, Ronald Reagan made use of this quotation and prefaced it with the statement that former Secretary of State Kissinger "is quoted as saying that he thinks of the U.S. as Athens and the Soviet Union as Sparta." But Kissinger denied having made such a statement, and Lawrence S. Eagleburger, a State Department counselor, called the quote "pure invention and totally irresponsible." According to *New York Times* columnist James Reston, the Kissinger quotation originated with Admiral Elmo R. Zumwalt, Chief of Naval Operations from 1970 to 1974. *Parade* magazine printed the quotation, Reston reported, and then "had the decency to publish a flat denial that Mr. Kissinger had said anything of the sort."[109]

❀ Knights of Columbus

BOGUS OATH "I do promise and declare that I will, when opportunity presents, make and wage relentless war, secretly and openly, against all heretics, Protestants and Masons, as I am directed to do, to extirpate them from the face of the whole earth; and that I will spare neither age, sex, nor condition, and that I will hang, burn, waste, boil, flay, strangle, and bury alive those infamous heretics; rip up the stomachs and wombs of their women, and crush their infants' heads against the walls in order to annihilate their execrable race. . . ."

The Knights of Columbus oath is one of the most famous of all the fake anti-Catholic quotes made use of by American bigots. In 1913, a special committee of Congress branded the "oath" as a fake, but it was used against Democratic candidate Alfred E. Smith in the 1928 presidential campaign, and against John F. Kennedy in the Democratic primary in West Virginia in 1960.

In spreading their message of ill will, American Catholic-haters have also used quotations from a series of fraudulent letters supposedly written by devout Catholics in Italy who seethed with hatred for Protestants. In one such letter, Monica O'Toole McNoonan, Regent, Mother of God Immaculate Nocturnal Adoration Society, is quoted as condemning "all . . . false heretical Protestants who attack the Holy Father in Rome and seek to destroy this Catholic nation. . . . The only schools in this country which honor God and the blessed Virgin Mother of God are the parochial schools of the Holy Roman Apostolian Church and not your atheistic Red-Communist public schools." Another letter, signed by Francis Xavier O'Toole, of the Society of the Immaculate Heart of Mary, Mother of God, rejoices in the ill treatment meted out to Protestant missionaries in Italy and warns Protestants: "Worse is in store for you as you will

soon find out. . . . You together with all other false heretics
and agents of evil will surely burn forever in Purgatory for
your damnable acts. You have absolutely no right to be in
Italy. The Italians are members of the True Church and they
don't need you lousy Protestant missionaries to confuse and
mislead them—so that you had better stay off of where you
don't belong." The names, the societies, and the quotations—
everything, in fact, except the hate animating the quote-
makers—are all fakes.[110]

🏵 Lawrence, James (1781–1813)

DON'T-GIVE-UP-SHIP QUOTE   "Don't give up the ship, boys!"

In June 1813, Captain James Lawrence, commander of the
U.S. frigate *Chesapeake,* engaged the British frigate *Shannon*
in battle and was mortally wounded. As he was being carried
below, he was supposed to have cried, "Don't give up the
ship, boys," and his words became a popular rallying cry in
the U.S. Navy during the rest of the War of 1812. But what
Lawrence actually said was more prolix: "Tell the men to
fire faster and not to give up the ship; fight her till she
sinks." In the end, the British hauled down the *Chesapeake's*
flag.[111]

🏵 Lenin, Vladimir Ilyitch (1870–1924)

ALL-SLAVE QUOTE   "The world cannot exist half slave and
half free; it must be all slave."

This sounds like Abraham Lincoln turned upside down, and
it is. And Wisconsin's Republican Senator Joseph R. Mc-
Carthy did the turning. In a speech in February 1953, Mc-
Carthy put these words into the mouth of the famous
Bolshevik leader and contrasted them with Lincoln's views.
Even so stout a defender of McCarthy as William F. Buckley,

Jr., acknowledged that the Wisconsin Senator had a habit of putting into direct quotes what amounted to a paraphrase of what he thought a person's position was.[112]

BEST-WAY-TO-DESTROY-CAPITALISM QUOTE   "The best way to destroy the Capitalist System is to debauch the currency. By a continuing process of inflation, governments can confiscate, secretly and unobserved, an important part of the wealth of their citizens."

People who quote Lenin on currency sometimes give a source: John Maynard Keynes. But in *The Economic Consequences of the Peace,* published in 1920, the British economist was not quoting Lenin. He simply remarked at one point that Lenin "is said to have declared that the best way to destroy the Capitalist System is to debauch the currency." Then he went on himself to point out that "by a continuing process of inflation, governments can confiscate, secretly and unobserved, an important part of the wealth of their citizens."[113]

CAPITALISTS-SELL-ROPE QUOTE   "The capitalists will sell us the rope with which to hang them."

There may be truth in the much-quoted remark that Lenin is alleged to have made about the capitalists' eagerness to sell their goods (the profit motive is, after all, unideological), but it is almost certainly a fake. Lenin was supposed to have made his observation to one of his close associates, Grigori Zinoviev, not long after a meeting of the Politburo in the early 1920s, but there is no evidence that he ever did. Experts on the Soviet Union reject the rope quote as spurious.[114]

CAPITALIST-TRADE-FINANCES-DESTRUCTION QUOTE   "When the capitalist world starts to trade with us—on that day they will begin to finance their own destruction."

This quotation, a variation on the capitalists-sell-rope quote, became popular among some anti-Communists in the 1970s, but it is equally spurious.[115]

CARESS-MASSES QUOTE "One would like to caress the masses, but one doesn't dare; like a dog they will turn and bite."

On February 7, 1965, *This Week,* a Sunday magazine supplement to the *Washington Star* and other newspapers, published an article by Robert Kazmayer entitled, "Lincoln versus Lenin," which Republican Senator Frank Carlson of Kansas read into the *Congressional Record.* Among other questionable quotes from Lenin appeared the caress-masses quote. It seems to have been a garbled version of something Lenin told Maxim Gorky after they had listened to a Beethoven sonata together: "But I can't listen to music too often. It affects your nerves, makes you want to say stupid, nice things, and stroke the heads of people who could create such beauty while living in this vile hell. And now you mustn't stroke anyone's head—you might get your hand bitten off. You have to hit them on the head, without any mercy, although our ideal is not to use force against anyone. H'm, h'm, our duty is infernally hard." It is difficult to understand why Kazmayer thought he had to improve on Lenin. The prospect of a world in which one cannot enjoy Beethoven until the arrival of a millennium in which everyone is a good Marxist-Leninist is actually even more dismal than the Kazmayer quote.[116]

CORRUPT-YOUNG-PEOPLE QUOTE "Corrupt the young people of a nation, and the battle is won."

This statement turned up in the *Dallas Morning News* for May 3, 1965, in a discussion of pornography. Lenin was supposed to have made the observation in 1922, but there is no evidence that he ever said anything as silly as that. The *Dallas News* quote was probably an adaptation of a phony

Lenin quote appearing in Kenneth Goff's ultra-rightest magazine, *Pilgrim Torch,* for February-March 1965: "Demoral-
ize the youth of the land, and the revolution is already won."
Apparently the phony-quote users don't even bother to quote
each other accurately.[117]

COULD-NOT-HAVE-COME-TO-POWER QUOTE   "If there had been
in Petrograd in 1917 a group of only a thousand men who
knew what they wanted, we could never have come to power
in Russia."

First used in the 1960s by the Christophers, a Catholic organization founded in 1945 to promote religious values in a
rapidly changing world, this Lenin utterance was news to
researchers at the Slavic and Central European Division of
the Library of Congress.[118]

FERTILE-FIELD QUOTE   "We will find our most fertile field
for infiltration of Marxism within the field of religion, because religious people are the most gullible and will accept
almost anything if it is couched in religious terminology."

In the late 1950s, evangelist Edgar Bundy, leader of the now-
defunct Church League of America, obtained this supposed
Lenin remark from radical-turned-reactionary Joseph Zack
Kornfelder (who may have made it up himself), and started
popularizing it. Soon it was going its merry way among
Protestant fundamentalists who deplored the liberal policies
of the National Council of Churches.[119]

FIREARMS-REGISTRATION QUOTE   "The first step in overthrow-
ing a government is to establish a firearms registration law.
After gaining sufficient strength, charge a suspected con-
spiracy, confiscate the weapons, and you will have neutralized
the defense of the people."

That Lenin, who died in 1924, had anything to say of use for
opponents of firearms-registration in the United States in the

late 20th century is highly improbable. It's as improbable as the "Rules for Revolution" (see Rules for Revolution), from which the firearms quote seems to have been taken and then expanded on. But it's been kicking around for years. In some American ultra-rightist circles Lenin comes close to being quoted almost as much as he is in the Soviet Union.[120]

FIVE-ENEMIES QUOTE "If you have five enemies, first ally yourself with four of them to destroy the one that is the most dangerous to you. Then ally yourself with three to destroy the fourth, and so on until you have only one enemy left, and you can take care of him yourself."

There is no evidence that Lenin ever made the five-enemies statement. Defenders of the John Birch Society, however, utilized it to warn "so-called liberals" that, by destroying effective opponents of Communism like the JBS, they would end up being destroyed themselves by forces to the left of liberalism.[121]

FREEDOM-OF-SPEECH QUOTE "Why should freedom of speech and freedom of the press be allowed? Why should a government which is doing what it believes to be right allow itself to be criticized? It would not allow opposition by lethal weapons. Ideas are much more fatal things than guns."

Lenin was no civil libertarian. A Russian Civil Liberties Union would have seemed as preposterous to him as the American Civil Liberties Union does to American reactionaries. But he never made the above statement, though Donald L. Miller, editor of *Freedom's Facts,* quoted it as "an old dictum of Lenin" in the September 1957 issue of his magazine. In April 1968, however, having learned that the free-speech quote was spurious, Miller reported that fact to his readers.[122]

GIVE-ME-A-CHILD QUOTE   "Give me a child for eight years and it will be a Bolshevist forever."

In his column for the *New York Times* on April 25, 1988, William Safire reminded his readers of what Lenin said about making babies into Bolshevists, but it is doubtful that Lenin ever made the remark. Ezra Taft Benson (President Eisenhower's Secretary of Agriculture) was one of the first persons to quote the child-for-eight-years statement. In a book entitled *An Enemy Hath Done This,* appearing in 1969, Benson gave as his source the testimony of FBI Director J. Edgar Hoover before the House Subcommittee on Appropriations on March 4, 1965, in which Hoover declared that Lenin had made the give-me-a-child statement in 1923. But no such statement appears in Lenin's writings for that year; by then a series of strokes had incapacitated him (he died in January 1924) and he did little writing. He did, though, tell young people in a speech in 1920: "You can become a Communist only when you enrich your mind with a knowledge of all the treasures created by mankind." The remark about children, with appropriate adaptations of course, has been attributed to Adolf Hitler as well as to Lenin, and to Catholic Church leaders as well. But there is no evidence that any of them made the statement, and its provenance remains uncertain.[123]

IMMUTABLE-AIM QUOTE   "Our immutable aim is, after all, world conquest. Soviet domination recognizes neither liberty nor justice. It is erected knowingly upon the annihilation of the individual will, upon unconditional submission to the work relationship as in other human relationships. We are, after all, the masters. Repression is our right. It is our duty to employ absolute severity and in accomplishment of such a task great cruelty can signify supreme merit. By employment of terror and its auxiliaries, treason, perjury, and the negation of all truth, we shall reduce humanity to a state of docile submission to our domination."

This sounds more like the ravings of a mad scientist in a Hollywood horror movie of the forties than a statement by the Russian dictator. In a speech to the New York Republican Club on July 12, 1960, however, Governor Nelson Rockefeller made use of the immutable-aim quote, which, it turned out, Rockefeller's research assistant obtained from economist Adolf A. Berle, Jr., who got it from "a Swiss scholar" named Claude Meyer, who found it in a now-defunct Swiss newspaper, and so on and on into obscurity. In pointing out the spuriousness of the quote, Abraham Brumberg, a specialist on Communism, noted that "world conquest" was scarcely a stated Communist aim, but that liberty and justice were. He also observed that the words, "we shall reduce humanity to a state of docile submismission," were far more ferocious than even Adolf Hitler allowed himself to be in his formal speeches. "Lenin surely has much to answer for," declared Brumberg. "And the system which Lenin helped to bring into being surely presents enough grave threats to the security of the world, enough transparent contrasts between its claims and its practices, enough evidence of duplicity, injustice and brutality for the most exacting and factual indictments imaginable. Hasn't the time come, then, to cease the petty prevarications, elaborate embroideries and the fanciful extrapolation?"[124]

INCONCEIVABLE QUOTE   "It is inconceivable that communism and democracy can exist side by side in this world. Inevitably one must perish."

Since Lenin considered Communism and democracy quite compatible, it is inconceivable he ever said anything like this. But the Gray Manufacturing Company of Hartford, Connecticut, used the quote in an advertisement in the *National*

Review in 1955, accompanied by the words: "Peaceful Co-existence. . . . BUNK!"[125]

INVECTIVE-SLANDER-SMEAR QUOTE   "Destroying all opposition by invective, slander, smear, and blackmail is one of the techniques of Communism."

Featured in one of evangelist Billy James Hargis's publications back in the 1960s, the invective-slander quote seems to have been as much Hargis's as Lenin's brainchild. Soviet experts at the Library of Congress could find "no information about this quotation." And Julian Williams, Research Director for Hargis in the 1960s, admitted that the quote "looks to be one of those occasions where someone made up a Lenin remark to fit one of Communism's tactics. Lenin just didn't spell things out that clearly." Fair enough.[126]

OVERRIPE-FRUIT QUOTE   "First, we will take eastern Europe, then the masses of Asia, then we will encircle the United States which will be the last bastion of capitalism. We will not have to attack. It will fall like an overripe fruit into our hands."

This particular quote—wording and punctuation vary with usage—has for decades been one of the most popular Lenin quotes ever to surface, and it was quoted by President Ronald Reagan in the spring of 1985. Years before, in an effort to track down its source, Harry and Bonaro Overstreet went through Lenin's *Selected Works,* but found nothing resembling the statement. Then they consulted people who were familiar with Lenin's *Complete Works* in Russian, and learned that research scholars at Stanford University had attempted to locate the "strategy" quote, as it is sometimes called, but without success. The curator of the Slavic Room of the Library of Congress, too, had labored in vain to authenticate it.
    Sometimes the date 1924 is given for the overripe-fruit

quote. But since Lenin died in January 1924, after a long illness, it is unlikely he said much of anything in 1924, and even less likely that he suddenly formulated a general plan for world conquest that year. In testimony before the Senate Internal Security Subcommittee on July 14, 1954, Nicholas Goncharoff, a Russian defector, apparently made the first use of the overripe-fruit statement, and it soon passed into general circulation. But when it appeared in *The Blue Book of the John Birch Society,* compiled by JBS founder, Robert Welch, in 1958, Louis F. Budenz, famous American ex-Communist, called the statement one of the "many questionable quotations from Lenin and Stalin that are floating around in ill-informed anti-Communist circles."

But the overripe-fruit quote continued to float. In May 1988, just before President Reagan left for a summit meeting in Moscow with Soviet leader Mikhail Gorbachev, a group of Soviet journalists interviewed him in the White House and one of them asked about the Lenin quotes. "Soviet specialists, as far as I know," he told the President, "in the American press and workers in the Library of Congress, qualified people, studied all the writings of Lenin and did not find one single similar quotation or something even close. Therefore, I'd like to ask you what you read from the works of Lenin and where did you get the quotations you've used." "Oh, my!" exclaimed the President. "I don't think I could recall and specify here and there. But, I've had a—I'm old enough to have had a great interest in the Soviet Union. And I know that in the things I studied in college, when I was getting my own degree in economics and sociology, that the declarations of Karl Marx, for example—that Karl Marx said your system, Communism, could only succeed when the whole world had become Communist. And so the goal had to be the one-world Communist state. Now, as I say, I can't recall all of the sources from which I gleaned this. And maybe some things have been interpreted differently in modern versions. But I know that Lenin expounded on that, and said that that must be the goal. . . . For example, here, in our Government, we knew that Lenin had expressed part of the plan that involved Latin America and so forth. And the one line that sounded very ominous to us was when he said that: 'The last bastion of capitalism, the United States, would not have to be taken; it would fall into their outstretched hand like overripe fruit.' " The quote itself was also surely overripe by this time; and will doubtless continue to fall obligingly into outstretched hands for years to come.[127]

PIE-CRUST QUOTE   "Promises are like pie crust, made to be broken."

Lenin did make use of these words in an article he wrote in 1905, but he was quoting what he called "an English proverb" (actually written by 18th-century English satirist Jonathan Swift) in order to criticize some of his Socialist adversaries in Russia. But the words were attributed to him and used widely as a Leninism in reputable, as well as disreputable, circles in the United States.[128]

ROAD-TO-PARIS QUOTE   "The road to Paris leads through Peking."

Lenin's supposed statement about Paris and Peking became popular in the 1950s. It was conservative California Republican Senator William Knowland's favorite quote. As his wife once explained: "In college, Billy studied Russian and came across Lenin's now famous sentence: 'The road to Paris is through Peking.' He pondered, and realized what this meant. . . . Most everything he has done since has been intended to block that road to Paris."

But there is no evidence Lenin ever made the Paris–Peking statement, though in 1923 he did declare: "In the last analysis, the outcome of the struggle will be determined by the fact that Russia, India, and China, etc., constitute the overwhelming majority of the population of the Globe. And it is precisely this majority of the population that during the past few years has been drawn into the struggle for its emancipation with extraordinary rapidity, so that in this respect there cannot be the slightest shadow of doubt what the final outcome of the world struggle will be. . . ." It is worth noting that after President Richard Nixon went to China in 1972 to lay the groundwork for establishing diplomatic relations between the United States and the People's Republic of China, the road-to-Paris quote gradually fell into disuse.[129]

SOCIALIZED-MEDICINE QUOTE "[National health insurance] is the keystone in the arch of the socialized state."

Early in 1949, when President Harry Truman proposed legislation providing for national health insurance, the National Physicians' Committee, bitterly opposed to Truman's proposal, came up with this kiss-of-death quote from Lenin to discredit it. In August, however, Democratic Congressman Andrew J. Biemiller of Wisconsin called the quote an "unwritten or unuttered quotation from an incorporeal source," and revealed that researchers at the Library of Congress, after an exhaustive search, had been unable to locate the statement in any of Lenin's public utterances and writings. Biemiller acknowledged that Lenin probably favored health, but he asked: "Does this mean . . . that because Lenin was for health, we must be for sickness?"

But the phantom quote, which apparently first appeared in Lawrence Sullivan's *The Case Against Socialized Medicine* (1948), continued on its way. It was used in a pamphlet, circulated in huge quantities by the American Medical Association, entitled *The Voluntary Way Is the American Way,* and it was quoted innocently enough by Governor Thomas E. Dewey of New York in 1949. (Dewey's citation led someone to remark: "The statement attributed to Lenin is not one of his. It is strictly Nicolai Dewey.") And in 1950, when Democratic Congressman George A. Smathers was campaigning in

Florida to unseat Democratic Senator Claude Pepper, the Smathers forces made use of the Lenin quote in attacking Pepper for supporting national health insurance. "Lenin said that 'the best way to communize any country is to socialize its medical profession,' " Smathers told his audiences.

Soviet specialist Abraham Brumberg, who has been tracking down phony Leninisms for years, includes the socialized-medicine quote in his list. "Ever since Communism has become a major preoccupation of politician and publisher alike," he once observed, "the world has been inundated with turgid passages of nebulous origin, nonexistent quotes from nonexistent books—as well, of course, as a host of sensational books about the Soviet Union which have been proved to be elaborate if clever frauds. . . ." Reputable scholars, Brumberg added, as well as people of integrity in the political world, have occasionally been taken in by some of these fake quotes.[180]

SPEND-ITSELF-TO-DESTRUCTION QUOTE   "We shall force the United States to spend itself to destruction."

On February 22, 1960, Ohio's Timken Roller Bearing Company placed an advertisement in the *Columbus Dispatch*, making use of this improbable statement from Lenin. The advertisement covered more than half an eight-column page and featured a picture of Lenin as well as the quote in large type. Curious about the statement, David Spitz, professor of political science at Ohio State University, wrote the Columbus office of the Timken Company asking for its source. From the superintendent of labor relations came a letter stating that the words came from a "literal translation of a speech by Lenin, made before the Soviet Presidium in 1919. It can be found in Volume 21, of Lenin's collected works." But not finding the quotation in either the English or the Russian editions of Lenin's works, Spitz wrote Timken again, asking for the specific date of Lenin's speech, the correct volume and page on which it appeared in Lenin's works, and the sentence in the Russian language of which the English quotation was a literal rendering. This time the manager of public relations for the Timken Company wrote him. "Our investigations into the subject," he said, "show that while Lenin may not have said verbatim 'We shall force the United States to spend itself to destruction,' the substance of what Lenin writes in Volumes 21 and 22 of his Collected Works amounts to substantially the same thing." In short: Lenin transubstantiated.[181]

TEACHERS-PROFESSORS-MINISTERS QUOTE "We must secure the good will of teachers and professors, of liberal ministers of religion and of the pacifists and reformers of the world in order to create a mental barrage in the minds of capitalist youth, which shall forever bar them from participating in a carnal conflict with the Communist order."

In 1956, the Senate Investigating Committee on Education of the California legislature came up with this goofy gem from Lenin, which, it was alleged, the Bolshevik dictator had issued as a "directive" in 1923. But Lenin neither thought nor wrote in this fashion; only an American would think in terms of "liberal ministers of religion." Researchers, not surprisingly, have never been able to locate the teachers-professors-ministers statement in Lenin's writings; and a consultant for the California Senate's Committee on Education admitted in 1970 that the quote was "spurious and perhaps a product of the McCarthy era. . . ."[182]

THREE-FOURTHS-PERISH QUOTE "What does it matter if three-fourths of the world perish, if the remaining one-fourth is Communist?"

Russian defector Nicholas T. Goncharoff, not Lenin, seems to have thought this one up, though of course he attributed it to Lenin. "It would not matter a jot," he had Lenin declaring, "if three-quarters of the human race were destroyed; the important thing is that the surviving quarter should be communist." Goncharoff, a former officer in the Red Army, was testifying before the Senate Internal Security Subcommittee on July 15, 1954, when he quoted Lenin to this effect, but there is no record of Lenin's ever having said this. But in various forms it pops up periodically in ill-informed anti-Communist circles.[133]

TURN-WORLD-UPSIDE-DOWN QUOTE   "Give me an organization of professional revolutionaries and I will turn the world upside down."

One has only to consult Lenin's *Collected Works* to discover that this is a distortion. In "What Is To Be Done?" (1902), Lenin criticized his co-workers for "acting as amateurs at a moment in history when we might have been able to say: 'Give us an organization of revolutionaries, and we will overturn Russia!' "[134]

USEFUL-IDIOTS QUOTE   "Useful idiots of the West."

Lenin, it is said, once described left-liberals and Social Democrats as "useful idiots," and for years anti-Communists have used the phrase to describe Soviet sympathizers in the West, sometimes suggesting that Lenin himself talked about "useful idiots of the West." But the expression does not appear in Lenin's writings. "We get queries on *useful idiots of the West* all the time," declared Grant Harris, senior reference librarian at the Library of Congress in the spring of 1987. "We have not been able to identify this phrase among his published works." It is ironic that in December 1987, when President Ronald Reagan, ardent anti-Communist, concluded an arms-reduction agreement with Soviet leader Mikhail S. Gorbachev, some of his former admirers began applying the Lenin phrase to Reagan himself. The President, hooted arch-conservative leader Howard Phillips shortly after the Reagan-

Gorbachev meeting in Washington, had finally become a "useful idiot for the Soviets."[185]

WIN-WESTERN-WORLD QUOTE "We will win the Western world for Communism without shedding a drop of a single Russian soldier's blood. How? . . . We will create fear, suspicion. We will work inside by creating national hatreds, religious antagonisms. We will pit father against son, wife against husband. We will inaugurate campaigns to hate Jews and hate Catholics and hate Negroes. . . . We will frighten them. We will create political chicanery. We will confuse international diplomacy. We will do these things."

To judge from this race-creed-color quote, Lenin had an agenda for the United States in the post-World War II era. At least his posthumous ghostwriters in the United States seemed to think he did when they stuffed these words into his mouth. Dallas's ultra-rightist crusader Dan Smoot enjoyed using the Lenin quote, without giving any source, when he served as moderator for billionaire H. L. Hunt's "Facts Forum" in the 1950s. But Lenin never thought inciting racial and religious hatreds was the road to revolution and he was simply not given to making fatuous statements like this one.[186]

❀ Lincoln, Abraham (1809–1865)

ALL-THAT-LOVES-LABOR QUOTE "All that loves labor serves the nation. All that harms labor is treason to America. No line can be drawn between these two. If any man tells you he loves America, yet hates labor, he is a liar. If any man tells you he trusts America, yet fears labor, he is a fool. There is no America without labor, and to fleece one is to rob the other."

Lincoln was supposed to have made this statement in a speech in Springfield, Illinois, on October 1, 1854, and it has been featured for years in labor magazines and at labor dinners. But Lincoln was not in the habit of calling people "liars" and "fools," and there is no record of his ever having uttered these words. Lincoln expert Paul Angle long ago dismissed the quotation as apocryphal, and Lincoln biographer Carl Sandburg once said that if anyone could prove Lincoln was author of the statement, he would go to Cleveland during a blizzard and "roll two peanuts around the bronze statue of honest old Tom Johnson," former mayor. He never had to roll the peanuts.

Lincoln did, though, make the following statement in a message to Congress in 1861: "Labor is prior to, and independent of capital. Capital is only the fruit of labor, and could never have existed if labor had not first existed. Labor is the superior of capital, and deserves much the higher consideration. Capital has its rights, which are as worthy of protection as any other rights. Nor is it denied that there is and probably always will be a relation between labor and capital producing mutual benefits.[187]

ANCIENT-SEA QUOTE   "The ancient sea of Venice, from Fiume to the inlet of Cattaro, uninterruptedly, through all of Dalmatia, ought to belong to Italy."

Perhaps the most amazing of all the Lincoln fakes was the ancient-sea statement appearing on the front page of *Popolo d'Italia,* edited by Benito Mussolini, on April 2, 1920, two years before his famous "march on Rome." Under the headline, "WHILE FIUME WAITS EXPECTANTLY," Mussolini's paper featured a translation into Italian of Lincoln's statement about the sea of Venice, followed by a letter, alleged to have been sent by Lincoln in 1853 to the Italian scientist Macedonio Melloni, calling for the unification of Italy and for a United States of Europe with Rome as the capital. The letter also denounced Great Britain for its "voracious greed" and declared that Rome "has given civilization to the entire world, which has actually discovered us, which has created us, redeemed us, educated us, and nurtured us morally with its indestructible laws. . . ." But Lincoln's main point—which was put in italics—was this: "The sea of Venice should be no longer defrauded. Not to concede its complete annexation, without exception of any sort, to Italy, is, for the citizens of all countries, and for the fellow countrymen of Franklin and of Washington, a true and real matricide, which would cast infamy upon the treacherous wrongdoers, and would cry out for vengeance to the Nemesis of history itself. You [Rome] were great when we were not even born." Lincoln's letter, translated into English, was reprinted in the *Philadelphia Public Ledger* in May 1920, dropped out of sight for a few years, and then reappeared in an Italian historical journal of some standing in 1931 and was at once repudiated as a forgery by both Italian and American scholars. In 1942, however, Mussolini's propagandists, claiming French-owned Corsica for Italy, quoted from the Lincoln letter in broadcasts to the Corsicans.[188]

ANTI-CATHOLIC QUOTE   "I do not pretend to be a prophet. But though not a prophet, I see a very dark cloud on our horizon. And that dark cloud is coming from Rome. It is filled with tears of blood. It will rise and increase, till its flank will be torn by a flash of lightning, followed by a fearful peal of thunder. Then a cyclone such as the world has never seen, will pass over this country, spreading ruin and desolation from north to south. After it is over, there will be long days of peace and prosperity: for Popery with its Jesuits and merciless Inquisition, will have been forever swept away from our country. Neither I nor you, but our children, will see those things."

These words, entitled "Lincoln's Warning," have circulated among Catholic-haters in this country since the late 19th century, but there is nothing of Lincoln in them. They were written by Charles Chiniquy, a Canadian-born priest who settled in Kankakee County, Illinois, in 1851, as head of a Catholic colony, and then abandoned his faith, began spewing out hatred for his former religion, and invented anti-Catholic utterances for Lincoln as part of his anti-Catholic campaign.

But Chiniquy did know Lincoln, though not very well. In 1856, Lincoln and Leonard Swett handled a case for Chiniquy in Springfield, Illinois, and years later, after Lincoln had become famous, the recusant priest falsely claimed he had been an intimate friend of Honest Abe and that the latter had secretly confided to him his fear and hatred of Catholicism. The false quote appeared in Chiniquy's *Fifty Years in the Church of Rome* (Chicago, 1886), a lengthy and bitter attack on the Roman Catholic Church.

Lincoln of course had nothing of the bigot in him, and the kind of views Chiniquy attributed to him where entirely foreign to his thinking. In June 1844, he wrote a resolution condemning the intolerance of the Know Nothing movement: "The guarantee of the right of conscience as found in the Constitution, is most sacred and inviolable, and one that belongs no less to the Catholic, than to the Protestant." And in a much-quoted letter to his friend Joshua Speed on August 24, 1855, he expressed his dismay over the bigoted views of the Know Nothings and warned that if they triumphed the Declaration of Independence would be corrupted into reading: "All men are created equal, except negroes and foreigners and Catholics."[139]

ANTI-PROHIBITION QUOTE   "Prohibition will work great injury to the cause of temperance. It is a species of intemperance within itself, for it goes beyond the bounds of reason in that it attempts to control a man's appetite by legislation, and makes a crime out of things that are not crimes. A prohibitory law strikes a blow at the very principles on which our government was founded. I have always been found laboring to protect the weaker classes from the stronger and I can never give my consent to such a law as you propose to enact. Until my tongue be silenced in death I will continue to fight for the rights of man."

Although Lincoln joined the Washington Temperance Society as a young man, avoided alcoholic beverages, and served cold water to celebrate his nomination as Republican candidate for the Presidency in 1860, the liquor interests in the United States have claimed him as a foe of Prohibition on the basis of the above statement, supposedly made in the Illinois legislature in 1840. Time and again, during wet-dry campaigns on the national, state, and local levels, the wets have made extensive use of the quote. But there is no record of the Lincoln pronouncement in the journal of the Illinois House of Representatives, and it appears nowhere else in any of his speeches and writings or in newspaper reports of his activities. According to Lincoln specialists, a leader of the anti-Prohibition forces in Atlanta, Georgia, fabricated the quotation in 1887, to persuade black voters to side with the "wets" during a local-option campaign.[140]

ANTI-SLAVERY QUOTE   "If I ever get a chance to hit that thing, I'll hit it hard."

Lincoln hated slavery and regarded it as incompatible with the principles on which the United States was founded, but he never made the above statement.[141]

BASEBALL QUOTE   "Keep baseball going. The country needs it."

During the 1930s and 1940s, CBS announcer Bill Stern was host for "Colgate Sports Newsreel," and made up all sorts of fanciful tales about athletes and sports events in order to jazz up his popular program. When Lincoln was dying, Stern announced on one program, he summoned a general to his bedside and murmured: "Keep baseball going. The country needs it." The general's name, Stern added dramatically, was Abner Doubleday, the "inventor" of baseball. There was of course no such deathbed scene; nor is there any real evidence that the Civil War general invented baseball.[142]

BOOTS-AND-BIBLE QUOTE   "I have never known a worthwhile man who became too big for his boots or his Bible."

Lincoln was said to have made this remark during the darkest days of the Civil War, but though he read and reread the Bible, and was deeply attached to it, there is no good evidence that he ever said this about it.[143]

BOUND-TO-BE-TRUE QUOTE   "I am not bound to win but I am bound to be true."

This sounds like Honest Abe, but honesty compels admirers of Lincoln to admit that there is no documentary evidence for the statement.[144]

CANNOT QUOTES
   "You cannot bring about prosperity by discouraging thrift.
   "You cannot strengthen the weak by weakening the strong.
   "You cannot help strong men by tearing down big men.
   "You cannot help the wage-earner by pulling down the wage
      payer.
   "You cannot further the brotherhood of man by encourag-
      ing class hatred.
   "You cannot help the poor by destroying the rich.
   "You cannot establish sound security on borrowed money.
   "You cannot keep out of trouble by spending more than you
      earn.
   "You cannot build character and courage by taking away
      man's initiative.
   "You cannot help men permanently by doing for them what
      they could and should do for themselves."

On January 25, 1949, Republican Congresswoman Frances P. Bolton of Ohio read these statements, attributed to Lincoln, into the *Congressional Record* and subsequently *Look* reprinted them, alongside a picture of the Civil War President and the suggestion that "it's about time for the country to remember" his advice. In February 1954, Arthur E. Summerfield, postmaster-general in the Eisenhower administration, included them in a speech he prepared for delivery in Akron, Ohio. But Stephen A. Mitchell, chairman of the Democratic National Committee, at once charged that Summerfield was trying to "put over a Lincoln hoax" with these quotations. "The entire passage is a fake," declared Mitchell. "Mr. Summerfield has put words in the mouth of the Great Emancipator that he never said. This quotation is intended to make Lincoln sound like a modern Old Guard Senator. It is another example of the Republicans trying to rewrite history." Mitchell insisted that the Lincoln aphorisms had all been exposed by Lincoln experts as forgeries.

Mitchell was right. In an article for the *Abraham Lincoln Quarterly* in December 1949, Roy P. Basler demonstrated that the Lincoln sayings were pure apocrypha. Congresswoman Bolton apparently got them from a friend who heard them on a broadcast by radio commentator Galen Drake on November 30, 1948. From Drake they were traced to the *Royle Forum,* house organ of a New Jersey machinery manufacturer. Said *Forum* editor Richard Cook, who had printed them without checking their authenticity: "One thing consoles me. I am now part of the Lincoln legend, and will live forever." Cook got them from some direct-mail advertising of another manufacturing concern which took them from a leaflet distributed in 1942 by the Committee for Constitutional Government, an ultra-conservative Washington lobby backed by New York State publisher Frank Gannett. The author of the "Lincoln maxims" was the Rev. William J. H. Boetcker, a Presbyterian clergyman who had given up the pulpit to lecture on industrial relations and who had published, between

1916 and 1945, several pamphlets containing these and other maxims which he had composed in order to further the cause of laissez-faire individualism. In the fall of 1942, the Committee for Constitutional Government distributed hundreds of thousands of copies of a leaflet entitled "Lincoln on Limitations," on one side of which was an authentic quote from Lincoln and on the other side a list of Boetcker's maxims, credited, in a footnote, to the "Inspiration of William J. H. Boetcker." The publication of Lincoln's and Boetcker's words together, however, caused someone—erroneously or deliberately—to attribute Boetcker's maxims to Lincoln. And despite Basler's exposé, they continue to be circulated as pronouncements of Lincoln.[145]

COMMON-PEOPLE QUOTE   "God must have loved the common people; he made so many of them."

There is, sad to say, no evidence that Lincoln ever said anything of the kind. It was James Morgan, in a book entitled *Our Presidents* (New York, 1928), who apparently first put words of this kind in Lincoln's mouth. According to Morgan, Lincoln dreamed one night that he was in a great crowd and heard someone in the crowd, surprised to see the President, exclaim in surprise: "He is a very common-looking man." Lincoln thereupon answered: "Friend, the Lord prefers common-looking people. That is the reason he makes so many of them." Over a period of years, the Morgan words were improved into the famous common-people quote.[146]

CONGENITAL-AVERSION QUOTE   "I have a congenital aversion to failure. . . ."

This doesn't sound like Lincoln, and it wasn't. It comes from a spurious letter from Lincoln to George F. Pickett and appears in Archer H. Shaw's *Lincoln Encyclopedia* (New York, 1950), along with several other apocryphal Lincoln quotes.[147]

CORPORATIONS-ENTHRONED QUOTE   "As a result of the war, corporations have been enthroned and an era of corruption in high places will follow. The money power of the country will endeavor to prolong its reign by working upon the prejudices of the people until all wealth is aggregated in a few hands and the Republic is destroyed."

The statement about corporations first turned up in 1873 and has been cited ever since in speeches, articles, and books by those with Populist and anti-trust sympathies. On December 15, 1931, Pennsylvania's Louis T. McFadden gave a speech in the House of Representatives featuring Lincoln's remarks about the crisis created by "the money power of the country." Two days later, however, Congressman Morton D. Hull revealed that he had been checking on the authenticity of the quotation and had concluded it was fake. To support his claim, he produced a letter from H. H. B. Meyers, director of the Legislative Reference Section of the Library of Congress, which informed him that there was no record of any such statement by the Civil War President. He also noted that Lincoln had lived and died before big corporations came into existence, and it would never have occurred to him to make such a statement. He reported, too, that John C. Nicolay, one of Lincoln's private secretaries, and, later on, with John Hay, one of Lincoln's biographers, had long ago pronounced the quote a forgery. The corporations-enthroned statement, Nicolay declared categorically, was "a bald, unblushing forgery. The great President never said it or wrote it, and never said or wrote anything that by the utmost license could be distorted to resemble it."[148]

DANGER-FROM-WITHIN QUOTE   "From whence then will danger come? If this nation is to be destroyed, it will be destroyed from within; if it is not destroyed from within, it will live for all time to come."

In a radio-and-television address in November 1953, Wisconsin's demagogic Republican Senator Joseph R. McCarthy, charging that the Truman administration had "crawled with Communists," quoted Lincoln on the danger from within. But McCarthy had distorted Lincoln's original statement in order to produce a point of view just the reverse of what Lincoln had expressed. In a speech in September 1858, Lincoln had stressed the love of liberty as the nation's greatest defense against subversion. "What constitutes the bulwark of our own liberty and independence?" he asked. "It is not our frowning battlements, our bristling seacoasts, the guns of our war steamers, or the strength of our gallant and disciplined army. These are not our reliance against a resumption of tyranny in our fair land. All of them may be turned against our liberties, without making us stronger or weaker for the struggle. Our reliance is in the *love of liberty* which God has planted in our bosoms. Our defense is in the preservation of the spirit which prizes liberty as the heritage of all men, in all lands, everywhere. Destroy this spirit, and you have planted the seeds of despotism around your own doors. Familiarize yourselves with the chains of bondage, and you are preparing your own limbs to wear them. Accustomed to trample on the rights of those around you, you have lost the genius of your own independence, and become the fit subjects of the first cunning tyrant who rises."[149]

DIVINE-SON-OF-MARY QUOTE   "But when I consider the law of justice, and expiation in the death of the Just, the divine Son of Mary, on the mountain of Calvary, I remain mute in my adoration. The spectacle of the crucified one which is before my eyes, is more than sublime, it is divine! Moses died for his people's sake, but Christ died for the whole world's sake! . . . Now, would it not be the greatest of honors and privileges bestowed upon me, if God in his infinite love, mercy, and wisdom would put me between His faithful servant, Moses, and his eternal Son, Jesus, that I might die as they did, for my nation's sake!"

In his memoirs, *Fifty Years in the Church of Rome,* published many years after Lincoln's death, Father Charles Chiniquy reported that Lincoln made the Son-of-Mary statement to him in an interview in the White House on June 9, 1864. But Lincoln scholars do not accept Chiniquy's book as a reliable source. And Lincoln himself (whom Chiniquy quotes, improbably, pages at a time) shared neither Chiniquy's hatred of Roman Catholicism nor his belief in the divinity of Christ. In his careful study of the Civil War President's religion, published in 1959, Dr. G. George Fox was impressed by the fact that "there are practically no pronouncements or even references to the Virgin Birth, the birth of Jesus, the crucifixion, the resurrection, the remission of sins through the blood of Jesus . . . and to the sacraments" in any of Lincoln's writings, public or private.[150]

EQUALITY-OF-BOTH-RACES QUOTE "How to better the condition of the colored race has long been a study which has attracted my serious and careful attention; hence I think I am clear and decided as to what course I shall pursue. . . . The restoration of the Rebel States to the Union must rest upon the principle of civil and political equality of both races; and it must be sealed by general amnesty."

These statements appear in a letter Lincoln wrote General James S. Wadsworth in 1864, in which he toyed with the idea of trading universal amnesty for the Confederates for universal suffrage for Southern blacks. In the 1950s and 1960s, civil-rights activists made much of the quote to refute claims of the Dixiecrats that Lincoln opposed racial equality. The letter, though, does not appear in the Wadsworth Papers in the Library of Congress. Crucial parts of the letter, moreover, which first appeared in the *New York Tribune* for September 26, 1865, have a shaky basis in fact. The *Tribune* gave the *Southern Advocate* for September 18 as its source; but historians have been unable to locate the newspaper. It is extremely doubtful that Lincoln ever made the equality-of-races statement, though he was unquestionably moving toward a generous civil-rights position toward the end of his life.[151]

FOOL-ALL-OF-THE-PEOPLE QUOTE   "You can fool all the people some of the time and some of the people all the time, but you can not fool all the people all the time."

Lincoln was supposed to have uttered these words when speaking in Clinton, Illinois, on September 8, 1858, while campaigning for the Senate against Stephen A. Douglas. But the *Bloomington Pantagraph* made no mention of the remark in its report of the speech, and it cannot be found in any of Lincoln's printed addresses. In a book *Lincoln's Yarns and Stories,* appearing around the turn of the century, Colonel Alexander K. McClure of the *Philadelphia Times* reported that in a conversation with a White House caller about the virtue of dealing honestly with the American people, Lincoln said: "It is true that you may fool all the people some of the time; you can even fool some of the people all of the time; but you can't fool all the people all the time." But McClure gave no source for his story. In 1905, nearly half a century after Lincoln's Clinton address, the *Chicago Tribune* and the *Brooklyn Eagle* attempted to prove the authenticity of the quotation by citing the testimony of witnesses, all of them past seventy, who expressed the belief that Lincoln had said something generally of this nature. Evidence for the quote remains extremely weak; but Lincoln expert Albert Woldman came to the conclusion that the epigram would probably continue to be accepted as authentic because it was "so Lincolnesque."[152]

GRANDSON QUOTE "I don't know who my grandfather was, but I am much more concerned to know what his grandson will be."

Lincoln might have said this, but there is no evidence that he did.[153]

HIGH-TARIFF QUOTE "I do not know much about the tariff, but I do know this much, when we buy manufactured goods abroad, we get the goods and the foreigner gets the money. When we buy the manufactured goods at home, we get the goods and the money."

People favoring high protective tariffs have made frequent use of this statement. In a three-volume tome, *The Industrial Development of Nations* (Washington, 1912), George Boughton Curtiss reproduced this Lincoln quote on one page under a picture of the Great Emancipator. Elsewhere in the book, he presented another version of the same idea: "Abraham Lincoln said: 'When an American paid $20 for steel rails to an English manufacturer, America had the steel and England had the $20. But when he paid $20 for the steel to an American manufacturer, America had both the steel and the $20.'" The second quote (of which the first was an adaptation) first appeared in the *American Protectionist*, New York weekly of June 29, 1894, and thereafter appeared repeatedly in the pages of the magazine. It was also included in the Republican Campaign Book for 1904; displayed conspicuously in the *Story of a Tariff*, published by the American Protective Tariff League in 1910; and used on a postcard distributed by "tariff reformers" in England in 1913.

Neither of the quotes cited by Curtiss can be found in Lincoln's letters and state papers; indeed, steel rails were unknown in Lincoln's time. In 1914, Harvard economist Frank W. Taussig, who served for a time as chairman of the U.S. Tariff Commission and who wrote the standard tariff history of the United States, revealed that both quotes were spurious, even though Lincoln began his career as a Whig and did favor a protective tariff. The *American Protectionist,* he reported, had picked up the quote from the *Harvard* (Illinois) *Independent* for June 9, 1894, which, in turn, took it from an oration on Lincoln delivered by Robert G. Ingersoll in 1891. Referring to Lincoln's tariff views in one part of his oration, Ingersoll made a short summary of the protectionist viewpoint, using the steel-rail example, which the *Harvard Independent* misconstrued as a quotation from Lincoln.[154]

KNOW-THERE'S-A-GOD QUOTE   "I know there is a God and that He hates injustice and slavery. I see the storm coming, and I know that His hand is in it. If He has a place and work for me—and I think He has—I believe I am ready. I am nothing, but truth is everything. I know I am right because I know that liberty is right, for Christ teaches it and Christ is God."

J. G. Holland's *Life of Lincoln,* published in April 1866, the year after Lincoln's assassination, reported that soon after Lincoln received the Republican nomination for President in May 1860, he sought out Newton Bateman, Superintendent of Schools in Illinois, to discuss the hostility of religious people towards his candidacy. During the conversation, according to Holland, Lincoln started weeping, and then delivered himself of the above statement about the divinity of Christ. But when William Herndon, Lincoln's former law partner, came across the passage in Holland's book, he was indignant. He knew that Lincoln, though religious in his own way, was not an orthodox Christian, and that he never talked the way Holland reported him as talking. So Herndon sought out Bateman, and Bateman told him what he had told Holland when the latter was gathering material for his book, and apparently there was some discrepancy in the two accounts. But Bateman swore Herndon to secrecy, for he did not want to get embroiled in a controversy over Lincoln's religious views. But Herndon, with the backing of other people who had known Lincoln well, convinced most people that Holland had put his own words into Lincoln's mouth.[155]

LOVE-JESUS QUOTE "When I left Springfield, I asked people to pray for me. I was not a Christian. When I buried my son [Willie], the severest trial of my life, I was not a Christian. But when I went to Gettysburg and saw the graves of thousands of our soldiers, I then and there consecrated myself to Christ. Yes, I *do* love Jesus!"

In 1883, Captain Osborn H. Oldroyd published a collection of stories about Lincoln, one of which reported that shortly before his death an Illinois clergyman asked him, "Do you love Jesus?" and he gave the above answer. But though the statement has been widely quoted, there is little reason to believe Lincoln ever said anything of the kind. Lincoln made many references to God in his public addresses, but very few references to Jesus, and, as his friend Jesse W. Fell pointed out, his lack of orthodoxy, "in the estimation of most believers, would place him entirely outside the Christian pale." Queried about the love-Jesus statement, Oldroyd said he didn't remember where he heard about it. He may well have taken it from a sermon preached by the Rev. W. W. Whitcomb, in a Baptist church in Oshkosh, Wisconsin, on April 19, 1865, right after Lincoln's assassination, and published in the *Oshkosh Northwestern* two days later. Whitcomb's sermon contained the love-Jesus statement; and several other Lincoln memorial addresses picked it up from Whitcomb's sermon. But it is highly unlikely that Lincoln ever said anything like it.[156]

PLAY-A-SOLO QUOTE "I will tell you *confidentially* that my greatest pleasure when taking a rest after splitting rails, was to play a solo on the jew's harp."

According to biographer Emanuel Hertz, Lincoln once discussed his love for music with a musical group called the "St. Marie Brass Band & St. Cecilia Society" and delivered himself of this confidentiality. But there never was such a musical organization and there is no record of Lincoln's ever having made the play-a-solo remark.[157]

POPULAR-SOVEREIGNTY QUOTE   "The nation must control whatever concerns the nation. The states or any minor political community must control whatever exclusively concerns them. The individual shall control whatever exclusively concerns him. That is real popular sovereignty."

For states-righters, the popular-sovereignty quote has been popular, but Lincoln never said these words, though he did say this: "The legitimate object of government is to do for a community of people, whatever they need to have done, but cannot do, *at all,* or cannot, *so well* do, for themselves— in their separate, and individual capacities. In all that the people can individually do as well for themselves, government ought not to interfere."[158]

PROUD-OF-CITY QUOTE   "I believe a man should be proud of the city in which he lives, and that he should so live that his city will be proud that he lives in it."

Lincoln probably would have regarded this sentiment as a truism, but there is no evidence he ever made the statement himself.[159]

TEACH-ECONOMY QUOTE   "Teach economy, that is one of the first virtues. It begins with saving money."

Here is another of the many Horatio Alger type of remarks put in Lincoln's mouth by some of his admirers. But it has as little basis in fact as the other Algerian remarks attributed to the Great Emancipator.[160]

UNSOUNDNESS-OF-THE-CHRISTIAN-SCHEME QUOTE "My earlier views of the unsoundness of the Christian scheme of salvation and the human origin of the scriptures have become clearer and stronger with advancing years and I see no reason for thinking I shall ever change them."

Atheists, agnostics, and freethinkers have for years made use of the unsoundness-of-the-Christian-scheme statement which they say appears in a letter Lincoln wrote "his old friend" Judge J. A. Wakefield in 1862. But no such letter appears in the scholarly edition of Lincoln's writings; nor is there any mention of Judge Wakefield in any of the multivolumed biographies of the Civil War President. Freethinker John Remsburg was the first to mention the statement in *Six Historic Americans,* published in 1906, but he gave no source for the statement. Lincoln was never an orthodox believer and he never joined the church. But his belief in the providential ordering of events increased, not decreased, as he became older, and his love for the Bible, particularly the Old Testament, was profound.[161]

WARTS QUOTE "Here I stand—'warts and all.'"

During the contest for the Republican presidential nomination in 1988, Vice-President George Bush, hard-pressed at one point, announced: "As Abraham Lincoln said, here I stand—'warts and all.'" But Bush was quoting Martin Luther and Oliver Cromwell, not Lincoln. It was on April 18, 1521, that Protestant reformer Martin Luther, excommunicated by the Pope for his heresies, exclaimed defiantly: "Here I stand; God helping me, I cannot do otherwise." And it was Oliver Cromwell, leader of the Puritan revolution in England in the 1650s, who supposedly told the artist who was painting his picture: "Mr. Lely I desire you would use all your skill to paint my picture truly like me, and not flatter me at all; but remark all these roughnesses, pimples, warts, and everything as you see me, otherwise I will never pay a farthing for it."

When *New York Times* columnist William Safire called the Bush headquarters to question the Lincoln reference, one of the Vice-President's speech writers moaned: "I goofed. All my fault."[162]

WRIGGLE-FOR-OFFICE QUOTE   "If ever this free people—if this government itself is ever utterly demoralized, it will come from this incessant human wriggle and struggle for office, which is but a way to live without work."

Office-seekers almost drove Lincoln out of his mind during his first weeks as President, but he never made the wriggle-struggle statement.[163]

❋ Long, Huey (1893–1935)

AMERICANISM QUOTE   "When the United States gets fascism, it will call it 100 percent Americanism."

This quotation, a slap at patrioteers, is a distortion of a statement that Huey Long, the Share-our-Wealth leader, made shortly before his assassination in 1935, to the effect that "when the United States gets fascism, it will call it anti-fascism," a slap at anti-fascist liberals. But the Louisiana demagogue never made the latter statement in so many words. It was writer Robert Cantwell who first reported that Long made the fascist–anti-fascist remark. But years later he told historian Arthur Schlesinger, Jr., that Long had not used those precise words in his conversation with him. Cantwell added, however, that the words represented the substance of what Long had told him.

In its anti-interventionist days before Pearl Harbor, the *Progressive,* a Wisconsin monthly, frequently quoted Long's anti-fascist remark to warn liberal interventionists that an anti-fascist crusade might end in fascism in America; in recent years it has been using the Americanism version of the

Long remark to warn conservative interventionists that an anti-communist crusade might produce fascism at home.[164]

Longworth, Alice Roosevelt (1884–1980)

BRIDEGROOM QUOTE "How *can* the Republican Party nominate a man who looks like a bridegroom on a wedding cake?"

Mrs. Longworth, Theodore Roosevelt's celebrated daughter, denied having made this remark when the Republicans picked New York's Governor Thomas E. Dewey to run against President Harry Truman in the election of 1948. "I didn't say it," she said flatly. "I wish I had."[165]

COOLIDGE QUOTE "Calvin Coolidge was weaned on a pickle."

Mrs. Longworth, noted for her acerbic tongue, has been credited with acidulous remarks she never made. The statement that President Calvin Coolidge looked as if he had been "weaned on a pickle" came from her doctor, who got it from another patient. "Of course, I repeated it to everyone I saw," Mrs. Longworth admitted.[166]

Louis XIV (1638–1715)

THE-STATE-IS-ME QUOTE "L' état c'est moi (I am the State)."

There's a story that the youthful Louis XIV strode into the Parlement of Paris in his riding costume, interrupted the debate, and proclaimed: "I am the State." There is no evidence that he ever did this, but he certainly believed the words attributed to him.[167]

❀ Maguire, William A. (1890–1953)

PRAISE-THE-LORD QUOTE   "Praise the Lord and pass the ammunition!"

When the Japanese attacked Pearl Harbor on December 7, 1941, Captain William Maguire, U.S. Navy chaplain, was reported to have uttered this famous battle cry as he pitched in to help the men on his ship carry ammunition up a narrow ladder leading to the guns. But Maguire (who had joined the Navy as a Catholic chaplain in 1917) didn't remember saying anything like that. "If I said it, nobody could have heard me in the din of battle," he said afterwards. "But I certainly felt what that statement expressed." Put to music by composer Frank Loesser, "Praise the Lord and Pass the Ammunition" became one of America's most popular World War II songs. But the slogan had already been used during the Civil War.[168]

❀ Mankiewicz, Herman (1897–1953)

GRACE-OF-GOD QUOTE   "There but for the grace of God, goes God."

Herman Mankiewicz, who did the screenplay for Orson Welles's *Citizen Kane* (1940), is supposed to have made this remark one day when he saw Welles crossing the *Citizen Kane* set. But Winston Churchill was credited with making the same sarcastic remark about Sir Stafford Cripps. And the original, unacerbic statement has been traced to John Bradford, 16th-century Englishman who, on seeing evildoers taken to the place of punishment, repeatedly exclaimed: "But for the grace of God there goes John Bradford." *Bartlett's Familiar Quotations* calls the 20th-century remark an "anonymous saying, attributed to Orson Welles, among others."

Maybe Welles, if he did indeed say it, said it about Mankie-wicz.[169]

❀ **Manuilsky, Dimitri (1883–1959)**

WAR-TO-THE-HILT QUOTE   "War to the hilt between Commu-nism and Capitalism is inevitable. Today, of course, we are not strong enough to attack. Our time will come in twenty or thirty years. To win we shall need the element of surprise. The *bourgeoisie* will have to be put to sleep. So we shall be-gin by launching the most spectacular peace movement on record. There will be electrifying overtures and unheard-of concessions. The capitalist countries, stupid and decadent, will rejoice to co-operate in their own destruction. They will leap at another chance to be friends. As soon as their guard is down, we shall smash them with our clenched fist."

Manuilsky, onetime head of the Third Communist Interna-tional (Comintern), is supposed to have made this statement, presumably in an unguarded moment, at the Lenin School of Political Warfare in 1931. But though it has been popular with opponents of peaceful co-existence with Russia since the mid-1950s, a thorough search in the relevant files in the Li-brary of Congress has failed to locate the statement. And there never has been a Lenin School of Political Warfare in Russia.[170]

❀ **Marie Antoinette (1755–1793)**

EAT-CAKE QUOTE   "Let them eat cake." (Qu' ils mangent de la brioche).

If the average American knows anything about French history (which is doubtful), he knows that Marie Antoinette said that

if the peasants didn't have bread to eat they could "eat cake."
But the remark, according to Columbia University historian
Jacques Barzun, is an old chestnut, current long before the
French Queen was born. In his *Confessions,* written in 1778,
French philosopher Jean-Jacques Rousseau wrote: "At length
I recollected the thoughtless saying of a great princess, who,
on being informed that the country people had no bread, re-
plied, 'Then let them eat cake.'" This was several years be-
fore Marie Antoinette is supposed to have tossed off her un-
feeling remark.[171]

❀ Marx, Groucho (1890–1977)

TRUMAN QUOTE   "This country would be all right if Truman
were alive."

When comedian Groucho Marx was reported to have made
this remark in 1947, Harry Truman (FDR's successor) was
alive and well in the White House, but regarded as a hope-
less incompetent by many Amercans. But Groucho was not
one of them. He vehemently denied ever having taken any
cracks at the Missouri President and in fact expressed his high
regard for him.[172]

❀ Mather, Cotton (1663–1728)

MALIGNANTS-CALLED-QUAKERS QUOTE   "There be now at sea
a ship called *Welcome,* which has on board 100 or more of
the heretics and malignants called Quakers, with W. Penn,
who is the chief scamp, at the head of them. The General
Court has . . . given sacred orders . . . to waylay the said
Welcome . . . and make captive the said Penn and his un-
godly crew, so that the Lord may be glorified and not mocked
on the soil of this new country with the heathen worship of

these people. Much spoil can be made of selling the whole lot to Barbados, where slaves fetch good prices in rum and sugar. . . . "

Cotton Mather, famed 17th-century Puritan preacher, disliked the Quakers, but he never said this about them. In 1682, the year Mather was alleged to have mentioned them in a letter to John Higginson, William Penn came to America to plan the colony of Pennsylvania as a refuge for Quakers. Penn visited several neighboring colonies before returning to England later that year, but he never made it to New England. The Mather hoax first appeared in Pennsylvania's *Easton Argus* in 1870; and though discredited by scholars, it continued to turn up from time to time in the 20th century.[178]

❀　Napoleon I [Napoleon Bonaparte] (1769–1821)

JESUS-NOT-A-MAN QUOTE　"I know men, and I tell you that Jesus Christ was not a man. Superficial men see a resemblance between Christ and the founders of Empires and the gods of other religions. That resemblance does not exist. There is between Christianity and all other religions whatsoever . . . the distance of infinity. . . . Everything in Christ astonishes me. His spirit overawes me, and His will confounds me. Between Him and whoever else in the world, there is no possible term of comparison."

The Jesus-not-a-man statement, which Napoleon is supposed to have made to General H. G. Bertrand during his exile on St. Helena, 1815–21, has appeared for years in various forms in books of spiritual uplift, but it is almost certainly apocryphal. The Frenchman who reported it, according to biographer Vincent Cronin, never even met the Great Conqueror. Napoleon did, indeed, believe in God and in an afterlife; he also thought morality rested on religion and retained a sentimental attachment to the Catholic faith in which he had been reared. But he "considered Christ merely a man," according to Cronin, and thought of the Gospels as "beautiful parables." Once, in a conversation about religion in 1817, he declared: "If I had to have a religion, I should adore the sun, for it is the sun that fertilizes everything; it is the true god of the earth."[174]

SHOPKEEPERS QUOTE   "England is a nation of shopkeepers."

It was Adam Smith, not Napoleon, who actually originated the shopkeepers remark. In *Wealth of Nations* (1776), Smith wrote: "To found a great empire for the sole purpose of raising up a people of customers, may at first sight appear a project, fit only for a nation of shopkeepers. It is, however, a project altogether unfit for a nation of shopkeepers; but extremely fit for a nation that is governed by shopkeepers." But during a meeting of the French convention on June 11, 1794, Napoleon heard Bernard de Vieuzac Barère quote Smith's phrase, and he later used it himself: "L'Angleterre est une nation de boutiquiers."[175]

❀ Nash, Ogden (1902–1971)

CATSUP-BOTTLE QUOTE   "Shake and shake the catsup bottle./ None will come, and then a lot'll."

The American poet Ogden Nash was celebrated for his humorous and satirical verse, and the catsup-bottle lines sound quite Nashian. In fact, though, they were written by one of his contemporaries: Richard Armour, the popular author of both humorous verse and whimsical prose.[176]

❀ Newton, Sir Isaac (1641–1727)

SHOULDERS-OF-GIANTS QUOTE   "If I have seen farther, it is by standing on the shoulders of giants."

For centuries Newton's admirers have quoted the shoulders-of-giants remark to show how modest the great English scientist was. Newton was far from being arrogant, but the statement (which he made in a letter to Robert Hooke, a physicist who challenged Newton's priority in inventing a reflecting telescope) was not original with him. It appeared in Richard Burton's *The Anatomy of Melancholy* (second edition, 1624), with which Newton was familiar, in a little different form: "Pigmies placed on the shoulders of giants see more than the giants themselves." And from Burton, the words have been traced to Bernard of Chartres in the early 12th century. It was even faintly foreshadowed six centuries earlier by the Roman grammarian Priscian.[177]

❀ Nixon, Richard M. (1913–)

GREAT-WALL QUOTE "This is a great wall!"

In 1972, when President Nixon's Chinese hosts took him to see the Great Wall, he is said to have remarked somewhat fatuously, "This is a great wall!" This was not his complete sentence, and out of context it sounds silly. It is only fair to put it back into its setting: "When one stands here," Nixon declared, "and sees the wall going to the peak of this mountain and realizes it runs for hundreds of miles—as a matter of fact, thousands of miles—over the mountains and through the valleys of this country [and] that it was built over 2,000 years ago, I think you would have to conclude that this is a great wall and that it had to be built by a great people."[178]

❀ O'Hair, Madalyn Murray (1919–)

STOP-RELIGIOUS-BROADCASTING QUOTE "If this petition is successful, we can stop all religious broadcasting in America."

In December 1974, two Californians, Jeremy Lansman and Lorenzo Milam, filed a petition with the Federal Communications Commission (FCC) asking FCC officials to freeze applications by all religious groups for TV or FM channels reserved for educational stations. At once indignant fundamentalist religious groups went into action. Blaming the notorious crusading atheist Madalyn Murray O'Hair for the petition, they flooded the FCC with protest letters quoting O'Hair as having announced: "If this petition is successful, we can stop all religious broadcasting in the United States." But Mrs. O'Hair hadn't made any such statement, nor had she filed any anti-religious petition of her own with the FCC. But in the late 1980s, petitions against the "O'Hair petition" to the FCC were still circulating, even though the FCC had denied the California petition years before on First Amendment grounds. "I think it's fabulous," laughed Mrs. O'Hair in the spring of 1988. "This craziness seems to have life everlasting."[179]

❋ Otis, James (1725–1783)

TAXATION QUOTE   "Taxation without representation is tyranny!"

These stirring words, frequently quoted as the rallying cry of the American Revolution, came from the mouth of lawyer James Otis, it is said, when he was arguing against British search warrants called writs of assistance before a Boston court in February 1761. But they may well have been the product of what historian Daniel Boorstin once called "posthumous ghost-writing." There is no contemporary record of Otis's having uttered the words. Actually they didn't turn up until 1820, when John Adams mentioned them in some notes he was making; and he may have been summarizing, not quoting, the gist of Otis's argument.[180]

✿ Paine, Thomas (1737–1809)

FIVE-BIBLES QUOTES "When I get through, there will not be five Bibles left in America."

Paine was a Deist, not a Theist, and thought the Word of God appeared in Nature, not the Scriptures. "The creation we behold is the real and ever-existing Word of God," he wrote, "in which we cannot be deceived. It proclaims His power, it demonstrates His wisdom, it manifests His goodness and beneficence." Paine was scornful of Biblical literalism, but he never made the five-Bibles remark. It continues to be popular, nevertheless, among religious fundamentalists who like to point out that the Bible has outlasted the author of the militantly Deistic *Age of Reason* (1794–95).[181]

✿ Pepys, Samuel (1633–1703)

MARINES QUOTE—"Tell it to the Marines!"

This appears to be an old folk saying whose origins are lost. But for many years a retired British Marine officer, presumably irked by the implication of gullibility on the part of Marines in the phrase, had scholars convinced that Samuel Pepys, the great 17th-century English diarist, first wrote these words, and that by them he meant that the Marines were wise and knowledgeable. It was Major William Price Drury of the Royal Marine Light Infantry who set this story in motion in his preface to a collection of stories entitled *The Tadpole of an Archangel,* published in 1904. King Charles II, according to Drury, told Pepys: "From the very nature of their calling, no class of Our subjects can have so wide a knowledge of seas and land as the officers and men of Our loyal Maritime Regiment. Henceforward, ere we cast doubts upon a tale that lacketh likelihood, we will first tell it to the Marines!" Years later, however, Drury admitted his story was a "leg pull of my youth."[182]

❀   Pershing, John J. (1860–1948)

LAFAYETTE QUOTE   "Lafayette, we are here!"

When General John J. Pershing stepped ashore in France as head of the American Expeditionary Force (A.E.F.) during World War I, he was widely reported to have exclaimed: "Lafayette, we are here!" But it wasn't Pershing who uttered these words; it was Lieutenant-Colonel Charles E. Stanton, chief disbursing officer of the A.E.F., whom Pershing had asked to speak for him at the tomb of Lafayette in Paris on July 4, 1917. "Many have attributed this striking utterance to me and I have often wished that it could have been mine," Pershing confessed. "But I have no recollection of saying anything so splendid. I am sure that those words were spoken by Colonel Stanton and to him must go the credit for coining so happy and felicitous a phrase."[183]

❀   Pétain, Marshal Henri Philippe (1856–1951)

SHALL-NOT-PASS QUOTE   "They shall not pass!"

In the winter of 1988, when Mayor Jacques Barat-Dupont proposed restoring Marshal Pétain's name to the slab in Verdun's council chamber which listed the town's citizens of honor, he ran into a torrent of criticism. "Pétain shook Hitler's hand," expostulated one indignant townsman, recalling Pétain's collaboration with the Nazis during World War II. "He deported people. . . . Oh, no, monsieur!" But Barat-Dupont insisted Pétain still deserved to be remembered for his services to France during World War I. In February 1916, he recalled, Pétain took command of the hard-pressed front at Verdun and revived French morale with his confident words: "They shall not pass!" The mayor was only partly right. Pétain held firm, to be sure (though at a tremendous loss of lives), but it was not he who cried, "*Ils ne passeront pas!*" It was his subordinate, Robert Georges Nivelle, a better phrasemaker, apparently, than Pétain himself.[184]

✾ Pinckney, Charles Cotesworth (1746–1825)

ANTI-SEMITIC QUOTE "For my part I never see any of the dirty fellows but that I would like to spit him on my sword. In less than 200 years if we admit them, the scurry scoundrels will be calling *us* their *ancestors*."

From the same source as the fake Benjamin Franklin anti-Semitic quote, this statement supposedly came from a diary kept by Pinckney when he was attending the Constitutional Convention in the summer of 1787 as a delegate from South Carolina. In the 1930s and 1940s, when American pro-fascists were making free use of the quote, they insisted that copies of the Pinckney diary had been destroyed when General William Sherman burned libraries in South Carolina during the Civil War. But there never was a Pinckney diary.[185]

MILLIONS-FOR-DEFENSE QUOTE "Millions for defense, but not one cent for tribute!"

When France, angered by what it regarded as America's pro-British policy, refused to receive Charles Cotesworth Pinckney as U.S. minister in December 1796, President John Adams decided to appoint a commission consisting of Pinckney, John Marshall, and Elbridge Gerry, with instructions to seek a treaty of commerce and amity with France. But in October 1797, soon after the commissioners arrived in Paris, three agents of French Foreign Minister Talleyrand (later referred to as X, Y, and Z, in the American mission's dispatches) visited the commissioners and asked for a U.S. loan and a bribe of $240,000. "Millions for defense," Pinckney was reported to have exploded, "but not one cent for tribute!"

But Pinckney denied ever having used those words. "No," he said later, "my answer was not a flourish like that, but simply, 'Not a penny! Not a penny!'" According to the *American Daily Advertiser* for June 20, 1798, it was South Carolina Congressman Robert Goodloe Harper who used the words attributed to Pinckney; he used them as one of sixteen toasts offered at a banquet in Philadelphia given by Congress on June 18 in honor of John Marshall on his return from France. But Pinckney got the credit, and the words became famous.[186]

❀ Prescott, William (1726–1795)

WHITES-OF-EYES QUOTE   "Don't fire until you see the whites of their eyes!"

If Colonel Prescott said this during the Battle of Bunker Hill on June 17, 1775, he was not the first to do so. Both Prince Charles of Prussia in 1745 ("Silent until you see the whites of their eyes") and Frederick the Great in 1757 (". . . no firing till you see the whites of their eyes") had made similar statements years before.[187]

❀ The Protocols of the Learned Elders of Zion

SHEEP-AND-WOLVES QUOTE   "The *goyim* are a flock of sheep, and we are their wolves. And you know what happens when the wolves get hold of the flock?"

This is only one of many quotes used for anti-Semitic purposes taken from *The Protocols of the Learned Elders of Zion,* one of the most widely circulating forgeries in modern times. The concoction of a Russian attorney named Sergis Nilus which first appeared in Russia in 1905, *The Protocols* purports to be the minutes of a meeting of Jewish leaders and freemasons in 1897 at which they planned to undermine Christianity and take over the world. During and after World War I, *The Protocols* attracted considerable attention in Europe, but fell into disrepute after the *London Times* published a series of articles in 1921 exposing the document as a forgery. But Henry Ford was taken in by it for a time, and Adolf Hitler made use of it in his campaign against the Jews. And, sad to say, despite the Holocaust, *The Protocols* continues to surface periodically, especially in Syria, Iran, Iraq, Saudi Arabia, and other countries in the Middle East.[188]

❀ Rabinovich, Rabbi Emanuel

NO-MORE-RELIGIONS QUOTE   "There will be no more religions. Not only would the existence of a priest class remain a constant danger to our rule, but belief in an afterlife would give spiritual strength to irreconcilable elements in many countries and enable them to resist us."

Both the quote and the quotee are fakes. Rabbi Rabinovich, like Israel Cohen (see Cohen, Israel), is a figment of the disordered imagination of longtime anti-Semite Eustace Mullins, a disciple of poet Ezra Pound. Mullins, it is said, has a sense of humor and doesn't take his own fabrications too seriously. But though exposed as fakes decades ago, Mullins's spewings continue to spread their poison in this country.[189]

REVEAL-OUR-IDENTITY QUOTE   "We will openly reveal our identity with the races of Asia and Africa. I can state with assurance that the last generation of white children is now being born. Our Control Commissions will . . . forbid whites to mate with whites. . . . Thus the white race will disappear, for mixing the dark with the white means the end of the white man, and our most dangerous enemy will become only a memory."

Another invention of racist Eustace Mullins, the reveal-our-identity quote appeared in Europe as well as in the United States, for during the 1950s Mullins sent the material "by Rabbi Rabinovich" he had made up to the Swedish anti-Semite Einar Aberg for distribution on a world-wide basis.[190]

❀ Reagan, Ronald (1911–)

MAN-HORSE QUOTE "There is nothing better for the inside of a man than the outside of a horse."

In December 1987, soon after President Reagan made this remark as he and Mrs. Reagan headed for the holidays to their ranch in California, people began pointing out that the statement was not original with him. Sherman Thacher, California educator, it was noted, had once opined: "There's something about the outside of a horse that's good for the inside of a boy." Dr. Cary Grayson, Woodrow Wilson's physician, had also made a similar remark: "The outside of a horse is good for the inside of a man." And going back even farther—for in history even precedents have precedents if you look hard enough—Lord Palmerston, 19th-century British statesman, it seems, had also made a man-horse observation. But the origin of the saying, one of Reagan's favorites, is unknown.[191]

SUMMIT-MEETING QUOTE "There is much that divides us, but I believe the world breathes easier because we are here talking together."

During a U.S.-Soviet summit meeting in Geneva in 1985, President Reagan was quoted by press secretary Larry Speakes as having made a couple of nicely phrased remarks to Soviet leader Mikhail Gorbachev during the course of their discussions about arms control. Not only did the President assert that "the world breathes easier" because of their talks; he also declared: "Our differences are serious, but so is our commitment to improving understanding."

Three years later, however, Speakes, now communications director for Merrill, Lynch and Company in New York, confessed that Reagan's summit statements were fakes. In his autobiography, *Speaking Out,* published in the spring of 1988, Speakes revealed that he had prepared the summit statements himself, because he thought Gorbachev's remarks to the press at the time were highly quotable and Reagan's disappointingly lackluster. He had asked one of his aides to make up some quotes, he said, and then polished them up and issued them as President Reagan's statements. In 1983, he also revealed, he had acted similarly. When the Russians shot down a Korean Air Lines jetliner, killing all 269 people aboard, he had "made Presidential quotes" out of Secretary of State George Shultz's comment about the incident transforming the U.S.-Soviet problem into "a Soviet versus the world problem."

Speakes's revelations touched off an uproar. CBS White House correspondent Chris Wallace, one of many reporters who had used the summit quotes, said he was "astonished, flabbergasted," while Marlin Fitzwater, who succeeded Speakes as President Reagan's spokesman in February 1987, called Speakes's fabrications a "damn outrage" and complained that they unfairly called into question the veracity of other Presidential statements. "Good God," exclaimed George Reedy, who had served as White House spokesman for Lyndon Johnson, "I would have been chewed up and spit out if I did that." He added that he knew cases of people "who wrote quotes for Presidents and had them approved before putting them out, but not with the guy never seeing them." President Reagan himself was reported to be "livid" over what Speakes had done, but in public he didn't seem unduly incensed. He had "no affection for these kiss-and-tell books" written by former White House aides, he told reporters, but he insisted that until Speakes's book came out he hadn't had the slightest idea that his former press secretary was making up quotes for him.

Speakes seemed surprised by the indignation his revelations produced. He knew Reagan's mind well enough to know that "these quotes were the way he felt," he said stoutly. "I was representing his thought, if not his words." In the end, however, he decided to resign his position with Merrill, Lynch and Company for fear of raising questions about the company's credibility. He also issued an apology. "To attribute to the President words not uttered by the President is wrong, period," he announced. "I have wronged President Reagan, a man whom I deeply admire and respect, and I have provided fodder for those who would aim the cannons of criticism at the President I served loyally for six years."[192]

❄ Reed, John (1887–1920)

THE-FUTURE-WORKS QUOTE   "I have seen the future, and it works."

American journalist John ("Jack") Reed, a radical, was in Petrograd (now Leningrad) in the fall of 1917 when the Bolsheviks led by Lenin seized power in Russia, and his eyewitness account of the event, *Ten Days That Shook the World* (1919), was filled with sympathy for the Bolshevik Revolution. But he wasn't the one who made the famous future-works statement about the Revolution. It was the old American muckraking reporter Lincoln Steffens, who liked to tell people, after visiting the Soviet Union: "I have been over into the future, and it works." Later he came to think that the system Mussolini brought to Italy worked pretty well too.[193]

❀ Reuther, Walter (1907–1970)

SOVIET-AMERICA QUOTE   "Carry on the fight for a Soviet America!"

In 1964 appeared John A. Stormer's little paperbound book, *None Dare Call It Treason*, a potpourri of distortions, misquotes, and spurious quotations, which featured a letter arguing "for a Soviet America" supposedly written by labor leader Walter Reuther and his brother Victor in 1934, when they were visiting Russia and studying the labor movement there. The "daily inspiration that is ours," they allegedly wrote, "as we work side by side with our Russian comrades in our factory, the thought that we are actually helping to build a society that will forever end the exploitation of man by man, the thought that what we are building will be for the benefit and enjoyment of the working class, not only of Russia, but for the entire world is the compensation we receive for our temporary absence from the struggle in the United States." Then, after more praise for Russia and more denunciation of American business, according to Stormer, the Reuthers concluded with the cry: "Carry on the fight for a Soviet America!"

The Reuther quote was a fairly old hoax. Time and again anti-labor Congressmen have inserted into the *Congressional Record* the letter from which it was taken, and it was a standard quote in right-wing publications in the fifties and sixties. But on September 22, 1958, Democratic Senator John L. McClellan of Arkansas revealed that not only were there three different versions of the Reuther letter in circulation, but also that three different versions of it had appeared in the *Congressional Record*. McClellan made it clear that the Senate committee probing labor rackets at that time regarded the for-a-Soviet-America letter as so questionable as not to be worth further consideration.

In *The Enemy Within* (1960), Robert F. Kennedy described his fruitless efforts to track down the incriminating letter when he was chief counsel for the Senate Labor Rackets Committee headed by McClellan. Mel Bishop, the man to whom the Reuthers were said to have written letters from Russia, explained that the letter had been written by Victor, not Walter, Reuther, and that around 1935 he had given it to his schoolteacher for safekeeping. But the schoolteacher, living in Pennsylvania in 1958, said she had never seen such a letter. Because of Bishop's unreliability and because there were so many "authentic" copies of the letter floating around, the Senate committee for which Kennedy was working did not take the Reuther quote seriously.[194]

❀ Rogers, Will (1879–1935)

NEVER-MET-MAN QUOTE   "I never met a man I didn't like."

In an epitaph for himself, Rogers put this remark in context: "I joked about every prominent man in my lifetime, but I never met one I didn't like."[195]

WEATHER QUOTE   "Everybody talks about the weather, but nobody does anything about it."

This statement is sometimes attributed to Will Rogers and sometimes to Mark Twain. Neither of them said it (see Twain, Mark).[196]

❀   Roosevelt, Franklin D. (1882–1945)

IMMIGRANTS QUOTE   "Fellow immigrants. . . ."

There's a story that FDR began a speech to the Daughters
of the American Revolution (D.A.R.) with the ironic words,
"fellow immigrants," but the story was too good to be true.
In a D.A.R. speech, Roosevelt did make the point that most
Americans descend from immigrants, but he didn't use those
precise words. Some reporter summarized his point that
way.[197]

NOTHING-WRONG-WITH-COMMUNISM QUOTE   "I do not believe
in Communism any more than you do but there is nothing
wrong with the Communists in this country; several of the
best friends I have got are Communists."

At the beginning of Chapter III in right-winger John A.
Stormer's *None Dare Call It Treason,* appearing in 1964, the
above statement by Franklin Roosevelt appears in italics.
Stormer gave the *Congressional Record* as the source for the
quote. The citation turns out to be an insertion into the
Record for September 22, 1950, by Republican Congressman
Harold Velde of Ohio of a long piece written by former
Democratic Representative Martin Dies of Texas, who headed
the Special House Committee on Un-American Activities in
the late thirties and early forties. In his article, Dies said that
Roosevelt made the statement to him in 1938. "Of course,"
Dies admitted, "I do not purport to quote the exact language
of these conversations. . . ." But he added: "Mind you, that
is a truthful account. He made that statement. Some of the
things I am telling you about I told the House of Representatives and published in magazines and speeches. . . . Although I published a book in 1940, no one sued me for
libel. . . ."

But Dies did not spring his FDR quote on the American
people until 1950; his 1940 book, *The Trojan Horse in*

America, says nothing about it. Why had he waited twelve years to make the revelation? The quote is exceedingly dubious; it is unlikely that FDR would have said anything like it, even flippantly, to the zealous HUAC chairman, though he may have told Dies he was exaggerating the size of the Communist movement in the United States. In the summer of 1936, FDR had several meetings with FBI Chief J. Edgar Hoover to discuss the activities of Communists and Fascists in the United States, and he eventually issued a directive giving the FBI charge of espionage and counterespionage in the Western Hemisphere. "For an administration that later was to be so virulently accused of being 'soft on Communism,'" commented Fred Cook in *The FBI Nobody Knows,* "Roosevelt and his aides seem to have been strangely alert to the dangers of Communist espionage."[198]

❁ Rules for Revolution

RULES-FOR-REVOLUTION QUOTES

"A.   Corrupt the young. Get them away from religion. Get them interested in sex. Make them superficial, destroy their ruggedness.

B.   Get control of all means of publicity and thereby:
1.   Get people's minds off their government from religion [*sic*]. Get them interested in sex, books and plays and other trivialities.
2.   Divide the people into hostile groups by constantly harping on controversial matters of no importance.
3.   Destroy the people's faith in their natural leaders by holding these latter up to ridicule, obloquy, and contempt.
4.   Always preach true democracy, but seize power as fast and as ruthlessly as possible.
5.   By encouraging government extravagance, destroy

its credit, produce fear of inflation with rising prices and general discontent.

6. Foment unnecessary strikes in vital industries, encourage civil disorders and foster a lenient and soft attitude on the part of government toward such disorders.

7. By specious arguments cause the breakdown of the old moral virtues: honesty, sobriety, continence, faith in the pledged word, ruggedness.

C. Cause the registration of all firearms on some pretext, with a view to confiscating them and leaving the population helpless."

A virtual cornucopia of crazy quotes for the cranky right to utilize as needed, the so-called "Rules for Revolution" supposedly originated in "the secret communist headquarters" in Düsseldorf, Germany, right after World War I, and came into the hands of two Allied military intelligence officers, one of whom was Captain Thomas Barber who said he had infiltrated the place. For some reason, however, the document did not surface until 1946, when it was featured in the February issue of a British publication, *New World News,* that year. Thereafter, the John Birch Society's *American Opinion* made much of it in the late 1960s, and so did far-right spokesmen Dan Smoot, Frank Capell, and Billy James Hargis. In the 1970s the National Rifle Association got into the act. In *The American Rifleman,* NRA organ, of January 1973, editor Ashley Halsey reported that Captain Barber, one of the intelligence officers who supposedly captured the Rules-for-Revolution document in Düsseldorf, had left a copy of it in his own handwriting before his death in 1962.

But the "Rules" is an obvious fake; it doesn't sound a bit like 1919. Respectable conservatives like William F. Buckley, Jr., M. Stanton Evans, and James J. Kilpatrick have all branded it a forgery; and an old anti-Communist newsletter,

116   *They Never Said It*

Combat, called it a "hoax on anticommunists." A careful search in the files of the FBI, the CIA, the Senate Internal Security Subcommittee, and the Library of Congress has failed to turn up any trace of the "Rules." The late FBI Director J. Edgar Hoover declared that one could "logically speculate that the document is spurious." Yet it continued to be quoted as an authority in the 1980s.[199]

❀ Scholz, Jackson (1897–1987)

OLD-BOOK QUOTE "It says in the Old Book, 'He that honors me, I will honor."

In the Academy Award-winning film *Chariots of Fire* (1981), Jackson Scholz, one of America's (and the world's) finest track athletes of the 1920s, hands a note to the United Kingdom's Eric Liddell, just before the latter took first place in the 400-meter dash during the 1924 Olympic Games, containing the spurious Old-Book quote. But the real Scholz (Olympic champion in the 200-meter dash that year) gave no such note to Liddell. "I'm afraid," he told reporters after the picture came out, "that my religious background was rather casual."[200]

❀ Sévigné, Marquise de (1626–1696)

HERO-TO-VALET QUOTE "No man is a hero to his valet."

This much-quoted remark is attributed to Mme. de Sévigné, but the famous 17th-century French letter-writer was only quoting a cynical remark she heard another witty Frenchwoman, Mme. Anne-Marie Corneul, make.[201]

❈ Shaw, George Bernard (1856–1950)

DEAF-DUMB-BLIND QUOTE   "All Americans are deaf, dumb, and blind."

When the great Irish playwright visited the United States in 1933, he encountered considerable hostility for a time because of his penchant for making satirical remarks about the American people. There was even a story making the rounds that when he met Helen Keller, the famous blind, deaf, and dumb woman, some years before, he had exclaimed: "Oh, all Americans are deaf, dumb, and blind anyway!" Shaw was angered by the story. Asked if there was a word of truth in it, he exclaimed: "Not a syllable! I met her at Cliveden when she was staying with Lady Astor. What I may have said, and probably did say after meeting her was, 'I wish all Americans were blind, deaf and dumb [the way you are]. We got on famously together. She didn't actually kiss me; but she smiled all over." Shaw resented the misrepresentation. "I tell you I have been misquoted everywhere," he complained, "and the inaccuracies are chasing me around the world."[202]

ONLY-INTERESTED-IN-MONEY QUOTE   "The trouble, Mr. Goldwyn, is that you are only interested in art, and I am only interested in money."

This much-cited Shaw remark comes from a much-embroidered version of Hollywood producer Sam Goldwyn's encounter with Shaw when Goldwyn visited him in England and tried to sign him to a contract to do screenplays. Shaw refused, but, apparently impressed by Goldwyn's insistence that he wanted to make films of quality, he teased him about his lack of commercial sense. Publicity director Howard Dietz then worked up a story that had Shaw say that Goldwyn was interested only in art and Shaw, only in money. As such it gained wide circulation.[203]

�֍ Sheridan, Philip (1831–1888)

GOOD-INDIAN QUOTE   "The only good Indian is a dead Indian."

In January 1869, according to Captain Charles Nordstrom of the Tenth Cavalry, the Commanche leader Toch-a-way approached General Sheridan, struck his chest forcibly, and announced: "Me, Toch-a-way, me good Injun." Sheridan gave him "a quizzical look," reported Nordstrom, and returned: "The only good Indians I ever saw were dead." Sheridan vehemently denied he had ever made such a statement, but the Nordstrom story persisted and gave Sheridan—and American whites in general—the reputation of being vicious Indian-haters. Sheridan, who became involved in Indian warfare after achieving distinction in the Union Army during the Civil War, regarded the Indians as savages and favored a hard-boiled policy toward them. But he insisted his Indian policy was "protection for the good, punishment for the bad," not extermination.[204]

✾ Sherman, William Tecumseh (1820–1891)

HOLD-THE-FORT QUOTE   "Hold the fort! I am coming!"

In the fall of 1864, when General Sherman was on his march to the sea and approaching the key supply depot of Allatoona, Georgia, he learned that the place was under critical pressure from the Confederates. Surveying the situation from Kenesaw Mountain, thirteen miles away, he sent off two messages to the Allatoona Union commander. One included the phrase, "hold out," and the other, "hold fast," and both contained Sherman's promise to arrive soon with relief. Later on reporters condensed the two dispatches into one message: "HOLD THE FORT! I AM COMING!" Sherman never actually used the phrase, "Hold the fort!", but it soon became a Union slogan and, later on, was made into a rousing revival hymn that swept the nation.[205]

WAR-IS-HELL-QUOTE   "War is hell!"

At a Grand Army of the Republic (G.A.R.) convention in Columbus, Ohio, on August 11, 1880, the great Union general declared: "There is many a boy here today who looks on war as all glory, but, boys, it is all hell. You can bear this warning voice to generations yet to come." Newspapers reporting the speech soon shortened his statement to the more stirring assertion, "war is hell," and it became famous. Queried about it years later, Sherman confessed he couldn't remember having said it, but he said he thought it might be an adaptation of a phrase he wrote during the Civil War: "War is cruelty and you cannot refine it."[206]

✿ Stalin, Josef (1879–1953)

AID-TO-BACKWARD-COUNTRIES QUOTE   "The Western nations must render aid to backward countries in order to socialize their economies and prepare them for entry into the world socialist system."

Apparently concocted in the early 1960s, the aid-to-backward-countries quote has been cited ever since in extreme-rightist circles to prove that "Stalin might be properly called the father of America's 'foreign aid' program." Who did the concocting remains obscure, but the citation itself is clearly a distortion of something the Soviet dictator wrote in 1921 in *Marxism and the National and Colonial Question:* ". . . the triumphant proletariat of the advanced countries should render aid . . . to the toiling masses of the backward nationalities in their cultural and economic development. . . . Unless such aid is forthcoming it will be impossible to bring about the peaceful co-existence and fraternal collaboration of the toilers of the various nations and peoples within a single world economic system that are so essential for the final triumph of socialism."[207]

BREAKING-EGGS QUOTE   "You can't make an omelet without breaking eggs."

Josef Stalin may well have made this remark to justify his tyrannical policies, but it was not original with him. It's an old saying, frequently uttered by people who have nothing in common with the brutal Soviet dictator. In a speech in Ocean Grove Auditorium while he was President, William Howard Taft told his audience: "We cannot make omelets without breaking eggs." Some authorities attribute the epigram to Robespierre in 1790.[208]

RIPE-FRUIT QUOTE   "Take eastern Europe, the masses of Asia, surround the U.S. by taking Africa, Central and South America, and we will not have to fight for it. It will fall into our hands like ripe fruit."

The fruit falling into Russian hands is sometimes ripe and sometimes overripe, and the fruit quote itself is sometimes Leninist and sometimes Stalinist. In 1986 a fundamentalist organization in Vernon, Alabama, called "Christ Is All," made Stalin the recipient of the fruit in its little leaflets.[209]

WORDS-AND-ACTIONS QUOTE   "Words must have no relation to actions—otherwise what kind of diplomacy is it? Words are one thing, actions are another. Good words are a mask for concealment of bad deeds. Sincere diplomacy is no more possible than dry water or wooden iron."

Stalin may well have believed this, but he never said it. Instead, what he said (back in the days before the 1917 Bolshevik Revolution) was, that when "bourgeois diplomats" prepare for war, they begin to shout "peace" and "friendly relations" and are not to be trusted. "A diplomat's words," in such cases, Stalin wrote, *"must* contradict his deeds—otherwise, what sort of a diplomat is he? Words are one thing—deeds something entirely different. Fine words are a mask to cover shady deeds. A sincere diplomat is like dry water or wooden iron." Stalin committed many horrible crimes, as even Nikita Khrushchev acknowledged, in his speech on the "Crimes of Stalin" in 1956, but that is no reason to put words in his mouth.[210]

❀ Sutton, Willie (1901–1980)

ROB-BANKS QUOTE   "I rob banks because that's where the money is."

According to the infamous bank robber himself, it was a reporter who thought up this smart-aleck remark and put it in his mouth.[211]

❀ Taft, Robert A. (1889–1953)

THE U.N. QUOTE   "The U.N. has become a trap. Let's go it alone."

This statement, attributed to Republican Senator Robert A. Taft of Ohio by extreme rightists who wanted the United States to quit the United Nations, is pure fabrication. Taft was critical of the U.N., but he never suggested abandoning it. In 1951, he wrote: "Entirely apart from any immediate threat of military aggression against the United States, I have always favored an international organization to promote the peace of the world and therefore of the United States." And on May 26, 1953, shortly before his death, he wrote: "I believe in the United Nations myself, but not as an effective means to prevent aggression. It does have many methods by which, through peaceful persuasion, it can deter and prevent war."[212]

❀ Talmud

CHEAT-A-GOY QUOTE "But it is permitted to cheat a goy, because cheating goyim at any time pleases the Lord."

This quotation is one of many fake quotes from the Talmud which anti-Semitic hate-mongers like Kansas evangelist Gerald Winrod, publisher of *The Defender Magazine,* liked to make use of. The correct text of course states nothing of the kind. According to Rabbi Ben Zion Bokser, a New York scholar and author of the pamphlet *Talmudic Forgeries,* the passage which was perverted by anti-Semites deals with the observance of the intermediate days of a festival; it specifies, among other things, that "one may collect debts, certainly if it be from non-Jews, on these days of *hol ha-meod,*" and "one may make commercial loans to non-Jews even where the would-be borrowers are new accounts." The passage, in other words, suspends certain restrictions upon commerce at the time of a Jewish festival, where the second party to a transaction is a Gentile. But anti-Semites have faked a quote in order to use an innocuous tradition to slander Jewish ethics.[213]

❀ Tocqueville, Alexis de (1805–1859)

NOT-A-SINGLE-BUREAUCRAT QUOTE "You know, in America someone sees a problem that needs solving. And they cross the street and talk to a neighbor about it. And the first thing you know a committee is formed. Finally, the problem is solved. You won't believe this. But not a single bureaucrat had anything to do with it."

President Ronald Reagan made gleeful use of the Tocqueville quote in a speech on November 11, 1982, but when critics pointed out that the word bureaucrat didn't exist in Tocqueville's day, a White House spokeswoman admitted: "The President changed it a little." Tocqueville's original statement: "If a stoppage occurs in a thoroughfare and the circulation of the public is hindered, the neighbors immediately constitute a deliberative body; and this extemporaneous assembly gives rise to an executive body which remedies the inconvenience before anybody has thought of recurring to an authority superior of that of the persons immediately concerned." It appeared in *Democracy in America* (1835), in a chapter in which the great French historian and political theorist discusses the way Americans rely on their own exertions to cope with the evils and difficulties of life.[214]

❀ Twain, Mark (1835–1910)

LILLIAN RUSSELL QUOTE "I would rather go to bed with Lillian Russell stark naked than with Ulysses S. Grant in full military regalia."

This remark, unfortunately, can be found nowhere in Twain's writings.[215]

SMOKING QUOTE "Giving up smoking is easy. I've done it hundreds of times."

Caroline Harnsberger's *Mark Twain at Your Fingertips* (1948), a compilation of Mark Twain's sayings, does not contain this statement, and it cannot be found anywhere in Twain's writings.[216]

THREE-KINDS-OF-LIES QUOTE "There are three kinds of lies: lies, damn lies, and statistics."

Twain didn't originate this pithy saying, but simply cited it in his autobiography. He credited it to Benjamin Disraeli.[217]

WAGNER QUOTE   "Wagner's music is better than it sounds."

It was not Twain, but Edgar Wilson ("Bill") Nye, who first made this remark about Richard Wagner's music. Twain enjoyed quoting it, but gave full credit to Bill Nye, a humorous writer and lecturer with many admirers in late 19th-century America.[218]

WEATHER QUOTE   "Everybody talks about the weather, but nobody does anything about it."

The famous weather quote first appeared in an editorial in the *Hartford Courant* for August 24, 1897: "A well-known American writer once said that while everyone talked about the weather, nobody seemed to do anything about it." Charles Dudley Warner, a journalist who collaborated with Mark Twain on *The Gilded Age* (1873), wrote the editorial, and he may have meant Twain when he attributed the remark to a "well-known American writer." But though Twain gave Warner the credit for it, it has been attributed to Twain himself ever since it first appeared, and in later years to Will Rogers. Twain's own weather remark went like this: "If you don't like the weather in New England now, just wait a few minutes."[219]

❁   Ulyanov, Vladimir Ilyich (See Lenin, Vladimir Ilyitch)

❁   Voltaire [Jean François Arouet] (1694–1778)

DEFEND-TO-THE-DEATH QUOTE   "I disapprove of what you say, but I will defend to the death your right to say it."

This is one of the most famous quotations from Voltaire and one of the most popular quotations among American civil libertarians. But Voltaire never uttered these words; and there is no reason to suppose he ever attempted to fight to the death for Claude Adrien Helvétius, the French philosopher on whose behalf he is supposed to have made his celebrated statement.

The origin of the quotation has been traced to a book published in 1906 entitled *The Friends of Voltaire,* written by S. G. Tallentyre, the pen name of Evelyn Beatrice Hall. According to Evelyn Hall, in 1758 Helvétius published *De l'esprit* (On the Mind), setting forth the idea that selfishness and the passions are the sole mainsprings of human actions and that there are no such things as virtues and vices. Voltaire was not impressed with the book; but civil and ecclesiastical authorities were highly incensed by it. The book was condemned by the Parlement of Paris, attacked by the Pope, censured by the Sorbonne, publicly burned by the hangman, and its privilege of publication revoked. In great distress, Helvétius insisted he had written *De l'esprit* in perfect innocence and hadn't had the slightest idea of the effect it would produce. Parlement finally accepted his *amende,* but deprived him of a stewardship which he held at the time and exiled him for two years to Vore.

"What a fuss about an omelette!" Voltaire exclaimed when he heard about the book-burning. Evelyn Hall's account of the episode concluded: " 'I disapprove of what you say, but I defend to the death your right to say it' was his attitude now." She did not say that Voltaire either uttered or wrote the statement; she simply summarized what she thought Voltaire's general attitude was and put it in quotes. Questioned about it in 1935, she explained: "I did not intend to imply that Voltaire used these words verbatim, and should be much surprised if they are found in any of his works."

The defend-to-the-death quotation, though spurious, probably summed up Voltaire's general attitude toward Helvétius accurately enough, and there was no desire on Evelyn Hall's part to mislead anybody.[220]

✿ Washington, George (1732–1799)

ANTI-JEWISH QUOTE   "They work more effectively against us than the enemy's armies. They are a hundred times more dangerous to our liberties and the great cause we are engaged in. It is much to be lamented that each state, long ago has not hunted them down as pests to society and the greatest enemies we have to the happiness of America—The Jews."

This quote, popular among American anti-Semites, is a distortion of a statement Washington once made about speculators in currency during the American Revolution. "This tribe of black gentry," he wrote, "work more effectually against us, than the enemy's arms. They are a hundred times more dangerous to our liberties, and the great cause we are engaged in. It is much to be lamented, that each State, long ere this, has not hunted them down as pests to society, and the greatest enemies we have to the happiness of America." Washington was, in fact, utterly without religious prejudice. When he visited Newport, Rhode Island, in August 1790, he had a friendly exchange with the Jewish community there in which he declared that Government of the United States "gives to bigotry no sanction" and "to persecution no assistance."[221]

BIBLE QUOTE   "It is impossible to rightly govern the world without God and the Bible."

Washington was baptized in the Anglican (later Episcopal) church, served as a vestryman, attended church fairly regularly, and believed that religion was the foundation for morality, but he rarely mentioned the Bible in his letters and public addresses, and never said, publicly or privately, that it was "impossible to rightly govern the world without God and the Bible." In notes which he jotted down in preparation for one of his speeches, he did say something about the Bible and human depravity. "The blessed Religion revealed in the word of God," he wrote, "will remain an eternal and awful monument to prove that the best Institutions may be abused by human depravity; and that they may even, in some instances be made subservient to the vilest of purposes." In the end, however, for whatever reasons, he decided not to make use of this statement, which is the only serious reference he ever made to the Bible.[222]

CAN'T-TELL-A-LIE QUOTE   "I cannot tell a lie."

The assertion that when the Father of Our Country was a little boy he told his dad he couldn't tell a lie is itself a prevarication. It's an innocent one all the same. It was put into circulation by an Anglican minister, Mason Locke ("Parson") Weems, a writer with a bent for hagiography, who wrote a biography of Washington shortly after the latter's death in 1799. When George was about six years old, Weems tells us, his father gave him a hatchet, and the boy at once hacked up a handsome young cherry tree belonging to the family. "George," said the father sternly, confronting the boy, "do you know who killed that beautiful little cherry tree yonder in the garden?" This, says Weems, was "a *tough question,* and George staggered under it for a moment." Recovering himself, though, he bravely cried out: "I can't tell a lie, Pa; you know I can't tell a lie. I did cut it with my hatchet."

The Great Confrontation Scene ends with a Great Embrace. "Run to my arms, you dearest boy," cries Washington's father, in transports, "run to my arms; glad am I, George that you killed my tree, for you have paid me for it a thousand fold. Such an act of heroism in my son, is worth more than a thousand trees, though blossomed with silver, and their fruits of purest gold."[223]

DEFICIT-SPENDING QUOTE   "Continued deficit spending must ultimately endanger all governments."

The Father of His Country would probably have been stupefied by the way the national debt skyrocketed during Ronald Reagan's eight years in the White House, but he never said anything in his own day about "deficit spending." The term, deficit spending, is strictly 20th-century, and not even Alexander Hamilton, Washington's Secretary of the Treasury, used it. But Hamilton did devise a plan by which the new Federal Government took over both the national and state debts left over from the American Revolution. And Washington approved the plan.[224]

DIE-HARD QUOTE   "Doctor, I die hard, but I am not afraid to go. Bring me the Book."

Shortly before he died at Mount Vernon on December 13, 1799, Washington is supposed to have asked for a Bible. But neither his doctors nor Tobias Lear, his private secretary, recorded any such request, and they were all with him at the end and wrote up his last moments afterwards. Washington did tell Dr. James Craik, "Doctor, I die hard, but I am not afraid to go," but he went on, not to request a Bible, but to add, "My breath cannot last long." But these were not his last words. Although he had difficulty speaking toward the end, he did manage to ask what time it was, urge the doctors to "let me go off quietly," and express some concern lest he be buried alive. "I am just going," he finally told Lear. "Have me decently buried, and do not let my body be put into the vault in less than three days after I am dead." Lear nodded dolefully. "Do you understand?" Washington asked in a faint voice. "Yes, sir," said Lear. " 'Tis well," breathed Washington. These were his last words.[225]

LORD-GOD-OF-GODS QUOTE   "The Lord God of gods, the Lord God of gods, He knoweth, and Israel He shall know; if it be rebellion, or if in transgression against the Lord (save us not this day)."

A little girl is supposed to have heard Washington utter this prayer on the eve of battle during the American Revolution, and Woodrow Wilson included it in his biography of Washington in 1896. But there is no evidence for Washington's ever having uttered such a prayer, and it is entirely out of character. Washington was a Deist, not an orthodox Christian, and though he belonged to the Episcopal Church and regarded religion as an important civilizing force in society, he simply was not given to outbursts of evangelical fervor.[226]

NOT-A-CHRISTIAN-COUNTRY QUOTE   "The Government of the United States is not in any sense founded on the Christian religion."

Freethinkers have made much of this supposed statement by Washington when he was President. But the statement was not Washington's; it was Joel Barlow's, and it appeared in the Treaty of Peace and Friendship which Barlow, American consul in Algiers, concluded with Tripoli on November 4, 1796. Eager to make it clear that Christianity was not an American state religion, and that therefore the U.S. government bore no official hostility toward Islam, Barlow included a clause in the treaty stating: "As the Government of the United States of America is not in any sense founded on the Christian religion; as it has in itself no character of enmity against the laws, religion, or tranquility of Musselmen; and as the said States never have entered into any war or act of hostility against any Mehomitan nation, it is declared by the parties, that no pretext arising from religious opinions shall ever produce an interruption of the harmony existing between the two countries."[227]

❀ Wellington, 1st Duke of (1769–1852)

AT-'EM QUOTE   "Up, Guards, and at 'em!"

At Waterloo in 1815, the Duke of Wellington was reported
to have shouted to his men just before the final thrust against
Napoleon: "Up, Guards, and at 'em!" But the Duke denied
he ever uttered that cry. What had happened was that at one
point, when the Guards were lying down, as they customarily
did under fire, when not actually engaged, he ordered them
to rise: "Stand up, Guards!" Then he gave the commanding
officers the orders to attack.[228]

PLAYING-FIELDS-OF-ETON QUOTE   "The battle of Waterloo
was won on the playing fields of Eton."

Visiting Eton many years after defeating Napoleon at Waterloo in 1815, the first Duke of Wellington is supposed in his
old age to have paid this tremendous tribute to his boyhood
school. But there is no reason to believe that Wellington ever
had much liking for Eton or that he would have dreamed of
tossing any bouquets its way toward the end of his life.

Who put the famous Eton remark into circulation? The
Count of Montalembert, a French writer who visited England in 1855, three years after Wellington's death, started
the ball rolling. He reported that when Wellington visited
Eton, where he had been a student in the early 1780s, he declared: *"C'est ici qu' a été gagné la bataille de Waterloo"*
("It is here that the Battle of Waterloo was won"). A few
years later the English writer Sir Edward Creasy published a
book entitled *Eminent Etonians* in which he wrote that Wellington passed the playing fields of Eton shortly before he
died and declared: "There grows the stuff that won Waterloo." In 1889, finally, Sir William Fraser amalgamated the
Montalembert and the Creasy remarks in his book, *Words
on Wellington,* and quoted the Duke as saying that the battle
of Waterloo was won on the playing fields of Eton.

But Eton didn't have any playing fields (or even organized sports) when Wellington was a student there. Nor did the Duke develop any particular affection for the place; in fact he was "lonely and withdrawn" there, according to biographer Elizabeth Longford, left before finishing his schooling, and didn't visit the place until thirty-four years later. And in 1841, when asked to contribute something to a subscription drive for new buildings at the school, he firmly refused.[229]

❀ Wilson, Charles (1890–1961)

GENERAL-MOTORS QUOTE "What's good for General Motors is good for the country."

Testifying before a Senate committee dominated by Democrats, President Eisenhower's Secretary of Defense, Charles Wilson, former head of General Motors Corporation, remarked: "What's good for the country, is good for General Motors, and vice versa." Almost immediately the Democrats pounced on the "vice versa," and turned Wilson's statement about General Motors's dependence on a viable economy into an arrogant statement about G.M.'s primacy in the nation.[230]

❀ Wilson, Woodrow (1856–1924)

BEAUTY LIMERICK "As a beauty I'm not a great star,
There are others more handsome by far,
But my face, I don't mind it,
Because I'm behind it—
'Tis the folks in the front that I jar."

President Wilson was so fond of quoting the beauty limerick that many people think he wrote it himself. But it was Anthony Euwer, a minor poet, who wrote it, and it was Eleanor

Wilson who first brought it to the attention of her father.
Wilson also liked the limerick about a Duchess and was mistakenly credited with having composed it too:

> I sat next the Duchess at tea.
> It was just as I thought it would be.
>   Her rumblings abdominal
>   Were simply abominable.
> And everyone thought it was me![231]

❀ Wise, Stephen (1874–1949)

COMMUNISM-IS-JUDAISM QUOTE   "Some call it communism.
I call it Judaism."

Anti-Semites have been fond of quoting this statement, which,
they say, Stephen Wise, prominent New York rabbi and
Zionist leader, once made. Actually, Rabbi Wise was a life-
long foe of Communism; and an official at Manhattan's Hebrew Union College, where Wise's papers are kept, reported
that no such statement appears anywhere in Wise's writings.
Even George Lincoln Rockwell, American Nazi leader, was
forced to admit that it was a fake.[232]

❀ Woollcott, Alexander (1887–1943)

WET-CLOTHES QUOTE   "I must get out of these wet clothes
and into a dry martini."

The martini remark sounds like New York journalist-actor
Alexander Woollcott, but he never made it. But his friend
Robert Benchley, the humorist, heard a press agent say it,
and he liked it so much he used it in one of the movies he
appeared in during the 1940s.[233]

❀ Zhou En-lai (1888–1976)

OPIUM-FOR-AMERICANS QUOTE "The more troops they send to Vietnam, the happier we will be, for we feel that we shall have them in our power, we can have their blood. So if you want to help the Vietnamese you should encourage the Americans to throw more and more soldiers into Vietnam. . . . We are planting the best kind of opium especially for the American soldiers in Vietnam."

According to evangelist Billy James Hargis's *Christian Crusade Weekly* for March 3, 1974, Zhou En-lai, premier of the People's Republic of China for many years, made these remarks to Egyptian leader Gamel Abdel Nasser in 1965, about the time the United States was getting heavily involved in the Vietnam War. Brian Crozier, expert on terrorism, has traced the statement to Mohamed Heikal's 1972 book, *Nasser: The Cairo Documents,* and believes Zhou actually made it. But it doesn't sound a bit like Zhou, and Heikal's book lacks documentation. American specialists on China, moreover, strongly doubt that Zhou ever said anything of the kind.[234]

❀ Zinoviev, Grigori (1883–1936)

RED-FLAG-OVER-WHITE-HOUSE QUOTE "The Communist International notes with great satisfaction that the work of the W.P.A. (Workers Party of America) for the past year has been expressed in a satisfactory broad and real revolutionary work. . . . We hope the Party will step by step conquer [embrace] the proletarian forces of America and in the not distant future raise the red flag over the White House."

In December 1923, when Soviet Foreign Minister Georgi Chicherin sent a message to President Calvin Coolidge sug-

gesting the establishment of diplomatic relations between the
United States and the Soviet Union, Secretary of State Charles
Evans Hughes sharply rejected the overture. The following
day the State Department released the text of "Instructions"
which Grigori Zinoviev, president of the Communist International (Comintern), supposedly sent the W.P.A., America's
tiny Communist Party, outlining ways to take over the country. "HUGHES REVEALS NEW RED ORDERS FOR AC-
TION HERE," reported a front-page headline in the *New
York Times;* "ZINOVIEV TELLS WORKERS' PARTY TO
AIM AT FLYING RED FLAG ON WHITE HOUSE."

Did Zinoviev actually send such "Instructions" to America's Workers Party? Soviet Foreign Minister Chicherin flatly
denied that the Comintern had done so; he denounced the
"Instructions" as a "clumsy forgery" and asked the United
States to submit them to an impartial international authority
for evaluation. In response, the State Department simply released the text of an article Chicherin himself wrote in November 1922 praising the work of the Comintern. But some
Americans were suspicious. In Congress, Idaho's William E.
Borah and Nebraska's George Norris asked to see the original, or at least a copy, of the "Instructions," together with
some evidence of their genuineness. None was ever forthcoming.

In later years researchers established the fact that the "Instructions" originated in the Justice Department's Bureau of
Investigation (predecessor to the F.B.I.) and were then transmitted to the State Department for use by Secretary Hughes.
But painstaking research in the files of the National Archives
has failed to turn up anything but the State Department's
press releases on the document. Even at the time, however,
Robert J. Branigan, an ex-Federal agent who had penetrated
the Workers Party for the Bureau of Investigation, strongly
doubted that Zinoviev ever sent a message of this nature to
America's little Red party. In an interview with the *New
York World* in November 1924, he declared: "The idea of

the Communist Party in America engaging in shooting practice and raising the red flag over the White House by armed revolution is a farce; there is a real radical menace, but it is not that. . . ." Comintern officials, moreover, were well aware of the fact that Federal agents like Branigan had infiltrated the Workers Party and they surely would have avoided sending out such inflammatory "Instructions." In any case, they took an exceedingly dim view of revolutionary possibilities in the United States in those days.[235]

Notes

1. Charles Francis Adams (ed.), *The Works of John Adams*, 10 vols. (Boston, 1856), X, p. 254.
2. Hesketh Pearson, *Common Misquotations* (London, 1934), 17; John Bartlett, *Familiar Quotations*, 15th ed. (Boston, 1980), 325.
3. Charles A. Jellison, *Ethan Allen: Frontier Rebel* (Syracuse, N.Y., 1969), 117–19.
4. "Armstrong Adds an 'A' to Historical Quotation," *New York Times*, July 31, 1969, p. 20.
5. Bent Corydon and L. Ron Hubbard, Jr., *Ron Hubbard: Messiah or Madman?* (Secaucus, N.J., 1987), 102–3; Donald Robinson, "The Far Right's Fight against Mental Health," *Look*, XXIX (January 26, 1965): 31; letter to John George from Edward Hunter, January 22, 1971.
6. *Brain-Washing: A Synthesis of the Russian Textbook on Psychopolitics* (Englewood, Colorado, n.d.), 27.
7. John Wesley, Sermon 93, "On Dress," *The Works of John Wesley*, 14 vols., ed. Albert C. Outler (Nashville, 1968), III, p. 249 and note.
8. Herbert Davis (ed.), *Pope: Poetical Works* (London, 1966), 81.
9. *Aesop's Fables* (Garden City, N.Y., 1968), 47; *Aesop's Fables* (Chicago, 1960), 20.
10. Proverbs 16:18.
11. Proverbs 11:14.
12. Proverbs 13:24; Samuel Butler, *Hudibras*, part II (1664), Canto I, 843.
13. *Sing-Song: A Nursery Rhyme Book*, in *The Complete Poems of Christina Rossetti*, 2 vols., ed. R. W. Crump (Baton Rouge, 1986), II, p. 42.
14. Elston Brooks, "Here's Z Reel Story on 'Razzamatazz,'" *Fort Worth Star-Telegram*, September 14, 1986, p. 29.
15. Bartlett, *Familiar Quotations*, 843; Tom Burnham, *The Dictionary of Misinformation* (New York, 1975), 255.
16. Tom Burnham, *More Misinformation* (New York, 1980), 52.
17. Letter to John George from U.S. Senator Don Nickles, January 10, 1983, including note to Senator Nickles from Mona Oliver, Congressional Research Service, Library of Congress.

18. Morris Rosenblum, "They Never Said It," *American Mercury*, LXII (April 1946): 496; "On Moving His Resolution for Conciliation of the Colonies," March 22, 1775, *The Writings and Speeches of Edmund Burke*, 12 vols. (Boston, 1901), II, p. 136.

19. *The Correspondence of Edmund Burke*, 10 vols., ed. R. B. McDowell (Chicago, 1958–78), VIII, pp. 127–33; William Safire, "The Triumph of Evil," *New York Times Magazine*, March 9, 1980, Sect. 5, p. 8; Safire, "Standing Corrected," *New York Times Magazine*, April 5, 1981, Sect. VI, p. 16; Bartlett, *Familiar Quotations*, ix; "Thoughts on the Cause of Present Discontents," April 23, 1770, *The Writings and Speeches of Edmund Burke*, 12 vols. (Boston, 1901), I, p. 526.

20. Samuel Butler, *Hudibras*, ed. John Wilders (Oxford, 1967), Canto III, line 547, p. 293.

21. Robert Atwan and Bruce Forer (eds.), *Bedside Hollywood: Great Scenes from Movie Memoirs* (New York, 1985), 74.

22. Rosenblum, "They Never Said It," *American Mercury*, 494; Dow Richardson, "They Didn't Say It," *New York Times Magazine*, January 7, 1945, p. 39; Richard Hanser, "Of Deathless Remarks," *American Heritage*, XXI (June 1970): 55–56.

23. Hesketh Pearson, *Common Misquotations* (London, 1934), 25; *History of Frederick II of Prussia Called Frederick the Great*, in *The Works of Thomas Carlyle*, 30 vols. (New York, 1858–65), XII, p. 339.

24. "Mitchell Would Modify '65 Voting Act," *New York Times*, June 27, 1969, p. 16.

25. Hanser, "Of Deathless Remarks," *American Heritage*, 56.

26. Mark Green and Gail MacColl, *There He Goes Again: Ronald Reagan's Reign of Error* (New York, 1983), 60–61.

27. "We'll Never Learn," *Kansas City Star*, January 15, 1986, p. 1B; undated letter, received, February 1986, by John George from Jim Hopwood, features copy editor, *Kansas City Star*.

28. Arnold Forster and Benjaim R. Epstein, *Danger on the Right* (New York, 1964), 29–30; *Congressional Record*, CIV, Part 12, 85th Congress, 2d Session, August 30, 1958, p. 16267.

29. *Wall Street Journal*, October 16, 1971, p. 1; Charles W. Colson, *Born Again* (Old Tappan, N.J., 1976), 57, 70–72.

30. Letter to John George from Abraham Brumberg, May 25, 1985; memo from Irene Schubert, Congressional Research Service, Library of Congress, to Senator David Boren, received from Senator Boren by John George, June 1985.

31. *The Mourning Bride*, Act I, Scene i.

32. Edward C. Lathem, *Meet Calvin Coolidge: The Man Behind the Myth* (Brattleboro, Vt., 1960), 151.
33. Ronald W. Clark, *The Survival of Charles Darwin: A Biography of a Man and an Idea* (New York, 1985), 196–99; Francis Darwin (ed.), *The Life and Letters of Charles Darwin*, 2 vols. (New York, 1896), II, p. 529; letter to John George from Larry Thomas, Research Editor, Jimmy Swaggart Ministries, November 4, 1985.
34. Donald Wilhelm, "What Happened at Wake," *Reader's Digest*, XL (April 1942): 41–46; Lt. Col. James P. S. Devereux, "This Is How It Was," *Saturday Evening Post*, CCXVIII (February 23, 1946): 10; Rosenblum, "They Never Said It," *American Mercury*, 493.
35. Eudocio Ravines *The Yenan Way* (New York, 1951), 265–66; Report of the American Bar Association Special Committee on Communist Tactics, Strategy and Objectives, *Congressional Record*, CIX, Part 15, 85th Congress, 2d Session, August 22, 1958, p. 19134.
36. Albert Lee, *Henry Ford and the Jews* (New York, 1980), 103; John Reeves, *The Rothschilds* (New York, 1887).
37. "Christianity and Revolution," *The Church Times* (London), April 13, 1923, p. 413; Robert Blake, *Disraeli* (New York, 1967), 204.
38. Sam Donaldson, *Hold On, Mr. President* (New York, 1987), vii.
39. Kenneth L. Calkins, "As Someone Famous Probably Once Said," *Wall Street Journal*, January 7, 1988, p. 14; "It's History Now, But It's Not Quite Correct," *Daily Oklahoman*, June 6, 1986, p. 35.
40. Keith A. Tosolt, Association Managing Editor, *The Digest of Chiropractic Economics*, to John George, October 29, 1987; Gloria Brueggmann to John George, September 1987; Wyn Wachhorst to John George, October 6, 1987; telephone call from Palmer College archivist Glena Wiese to John George, September 1987.
41. *New York Herald Tribune*, October 18, 1964.
42. "Self-Reliance," *The Collected Works of Ralph Waldo Emerson* (Cambridge, Mass., 1979), II, p. 33.
43. Sarah B. Yule and Mary S. Kenne, *Borrowings: A Collection of Helpful and Beautiful Thoughts* (New York, 1889), 52; *Journals of Ralph Waldo Emerson*, 10 vols. (Boston and New York, 1912), VIII, p. 528.
44. Calkins, "As Someone Famous Probably Once Said," *Wall Street Journal*, p. 14.
45. Burnham, *Dictionary of Misinformation*, 123.
46. Rosenblum, "They Never Said It," *American Mercury*, 495; Matthew Josephson, *The Robber Barons* (New York, 1934), 141.
47. Ralph Lord Roy, *Apostles of Discord* (Boston, 1953), 77–78; Mar-

garet Hartley, "The Subliterature of Hate," *Southwest Review* (Summer 1952), 188; Arnold Forster and Benjamin Epstein, *The Trouble-Makers* (New York, 1952), 148n.

48. Ibid.
49. "The Case of Billy Sunday, His Arraignment on Serious Charges, and Self Conviction of Guilt," (published by the Truth Seeker Co., 62 Vesey St., New York, n.d., 32 pp.)
50. Samuel T. Pickard, *Life and Letters of John Greenleaf Whittier*, 2 vols. (London, 1895), I, pp. 454–57.
51. Tax-Exempt Foundations, Hearings, 82nd Congress, 2d Session, on House Resolution 561, November 18–December 30, 1952; *John Birch Society Bulletin*, February 1971, September 1973; Robert Welch, *Wild Statements* (1965); letter to John George from Richard Magat, Director, Office of Reports, The Ford Foundation, July 16, 1970.
52. Rosenblum, "They Never Said It," *American Mercury*, 494; Hanser, "Of Deathless Remarks," *American Heritage*, 56; Bartlett, *Familiar Quotations*, attributes the statement to Abbe Irailh, *Querelles litteraires* (1961), 183.
53. Paul F. Boller, Jr., and Ronald L. Davis, *Hollywood Anecdotes* (New York, 1987), 38–39.
54. Allen Peskin, *Garfield* (Kent State University Press, 1978), 505–10.
55. William R. Balch, *The Life of James Abram Garfield* (Philadelphia, 1881), 270–73; John M. Taylor, *Garfield of Ohio* (New York, 1970), 103.
56. "Gaullist Apocrypha," *National Review*, XIII (November 6, 1962): 346.
57. Robert E. Sherwood, *Roosevelt and Hopkins: An Intimate History* (New York, 1948), 686, 691, 956; *The Memoirs of Cordell Hull*, 2 vols. (New York, 1948), II, p. 1208; Orville H. Bullitt (ed.), *For the President, Personal and Secret: Correspondence between Franklin D. Roosevelt and William C. Bullitt* (Boston, 1972), 568; Milton Viorst, *Hostile Allies: FDR and Charles DeGaulle* (New York, 1965), 146–47.
58. C. V. Wedgwood, *Edward Gibbon* (London, 1955), 418–19.
59. Steven V. Roberts, "Return to the Land of the Gipper," *New York Times*, Washington, March 9, 1988, p. 14; Garry Wills, *Reagan's America* (New York, 1987), 143, 511.
60. Thomas Vinciguerra, "Culture Didn't Make Goering Go for His Gun," *New York Times*, September 17, 1987, p. 22; Bartlett, *Familiar Quotations*, 816; *"Wenn ich Kultur höre . . . entsichereich meinen Browning."*

61. Stephen Shadegg, *Barry Goldwater: Freedom Is His Official Flight Plan* (New York, 1962), 277n.
62. Arthur Marx, *Goldwyn: A Biography of the Man Behind the Myth* (New York, 1976), 298.
63. Marx, *Goldwyn*, 322.
64. Carol Easton, *The Search for Sam Goldwyn* (New York, 1976), 150.
65. Ibid.
66. Marx, *Goldwyn*, 270.
67. Norman Zierold, *The Moguls* (New York, 1969), 127.
68. Marx, *Goldwyn*, 10; Zierold, *Moguls*, 127.
69. Marx, *Goldwyn*, 10.
70. Zierold, *Moguls*, 127.
71. Ibid.
72. Marx, *Goldwyn*, 9–10; Zierold, *Moguls*, 129.
73. Easton, *Search for Goldwyn*, 150.
74. Marx, *Goldwyn*, 210.
75. Zierold, *Moguls*, 129.
76. Zierold, *Moguls*, 127–28; Boller and Davis, *Hollywood Anecdotes*, 94.
77. Easton, *Search for Goldwyn*, 150.
78. Ibid.
79. Zierold, *Moguls*, 128.
80. Ibid.; Easton, *Search for Goldwyn*, 150.
81. *Free Inquiry* (Winter 1980/81), 22; Sol Gardon and Judith Gordon, *Raising a Child Conservatively in a Sexually Permissive World* (New York, 1983); *The Unbelievable Truth About Your Public Schools* (Buffalo, N.Y., 1980); *Did the Sun Shine Before You Were Born? A Sex Education Primer* (Fayetteville, N.Y., 1974).
82. Richardson, "They Didn't Say It," 39; Burnham, *Dictionary of Misinformation*, 98.
83. Roy Paul Nelson, "On Cranberries and Communism," *Christian Century*, LXXXIX (March 21, 1962): 356–59.
84. Morris Kominsky, *The Hoaxers* (Boston, 1970), 117–19.
85. Letter to John George from Joachim Schonbeck, Acting Press Counselor, West German Embassy, August 14, 1970, stating that the Institute for Contemporary History was unable to verify the Hitler quote; John George phone conversation with Sidney Hook, January 31, 1988; Sidney Hook, *Out of Step: An Unquiet Life in the Twentieth Century* (New York, 1987), 558.
86. Mark Green and Gail MacColl, *There He Goes Again: Ronald Reagan's Reign of Error* (New York, 1983), 61.
87. Burnham, *Dictionary of Misinformation*, 227.
88. Hanser, "Of Deathless Remarks," 56.

89. Edward Angly, *Oh, Yeah?* (New York, 1932), 17.

90. Robert Sherwood, *Roosevelt and Hopkins: An Intimate History* (New York, 1948), 61; Sherwin D. Smith, "Boondoggle That Helped 38 Million People," *New York Times Magazine,* May 2, 1965, pp. 74–76.

91. Smith, "Boondoggle," 37; Sherwood, *Roosevelt and Hopkins,* 102–3.

92. Stephen Wermiel, "For a Quotable High Court View, Never Let Facts Stand in the Way," *Wall Street Journal,* January 31, 1986.

93. *Pat Robertson's Perspective* (Fall 1981), CBN, Virginia Beach, Virginia 23463; Paul Kurtz, *In Defense of Secular Humanism* (Buffalo, N.Y., 1983), 43.

94. Green and MacColl, *There He Goes Again,* 95; "Reagan Says Many New Dealers Wanted Fascism," *New York Times,* December 23, 1981, p. A12.

95. *The Letters of Robert G. Ingersoll,* ed. Eva Ingersoll Wakefield (New York, 1951), 279–80; George Seldes, *The Great Quotations* (New York, 1960), 16–17.

96. Marquis James, *Andrew Jackson: Portrait of a President* (Indianapolis, 1937), 304; Robert V. Remini, *Andrew Jackson and the Course of American Freedom, 1822–1832* (New York, 1981), 276–77.

97. Rena G. Kunis, "One Man's Majority," *New York Times,* October 25, 1987, p. 22.

98. Helen C. Drummond, "Spoils System," *New York Times,* September 2, 1951, Section VI, p. 4; Ivor Debenham Spencer, *The Victor and the Spoils: A Life of William L. Marcy* (Providence, R.I., 1959), 59–61.

99. Martin Tolchink, "Nothing Like Bogus Guidance on Japanese Intent," *New York Times,* January 6, 1988, p. 10.

100. William F. Buckley, Jr., "Beware the Rising Banner of Big Brother," *New York Daily News,* November 11, 1987, p. 31; Henry Thoreau, "Civil Disobedience," *Walden and Other Writings,* ed. Brooks Atkinson (New York, 1937), 635.

101. Kenneth L. Calkins, "As Someone Famous Probably Once Said . . . ," *Wall Street Journal,* January 7, 1988, p. 14.

102. Hanser, "Of Deathless Remarks," 55.

103. I. Bernard Cohen, *Revolution in Science* (Cambridge, Mass., 1985), 237–44.

104. Abraham Brumberg, "Apropos of Quotation Mongering," *New Republic,* CXLIII (August 29, 1960): 15–16.

105. July 26, 1961, *Congressional Record,* Vol. 107, Part II, 87th Congress, 1st Session, p. 13608; Donald Janson, "Communist Rules for

Revolt Viewed as Durable Fraud," *New York Times,* July 10, 1970, Part I, p. 30; *Congressional Record,* Vol. 108, Part III, 87th Congress, 2d Session, March 8, 1962, p. 3676.

106. Robert L. Preston, *Wake Up America* (Salt Lake City, 1972), 16; Ezra Taft Benson, *An Enemy Hath Done This* (Salt Lake City, 1969), 320.
107. Lawrence Thompson (ed.), *Selected Letters of Robert Frost* (New York, 1964), 593–95; Franklin D. Reeve, *Robert Frost in Russia* (Boston, 1964), 120–33.
108. Kominsky, *Hoaxers,* 519–21.
109. Green and MacColl, *There He Goes Again,* 36–37; "Reagan Appeals for Wide Support," *New York Times,* April 1, 1976, p. 22.
110. Theodore C. Sorensen, *Kennedy* (New York, 1965), 144.
111. Glenn Tucker, *Poltroons and Patriots: A Popular Account of the War of 1812,* 2 vols. (Indianapolis, 1954), I, pp. 267, 269.
112. William F. Buckley, Jr., and Brent Bozell, *McCarthy and His Enemies* (Chicago, 1954), 90 and note.
113. John Maynard Keynes, *The Economic Consequences of the Peace* (New York, 1920), 235.
114. William Safire, "As Lenin May or May Not Have Said," *New York Times* News Service, April 29, 1987; letters to John George from Abraham Brumberg, May 25, 1985, from Arnaud de Borchgrave, April 24, 1983, and from Arnold Beichman, July 19, 1987.
115. Ibid.
116. Christopher Hill, *Lenin and the Russian Revolution* (London, 1947), 220; Kominsky, *Hoaxers,* 50–53.
117. Kominsky, *Hoaxers,* 420.
118. Kominsky, *Hoaxers,* 46–47.
119. Kominsky, *Hoaxers,* 42–45; Tom Anderson, "Straight Talk," *Farm and Ranch,* XC (August 1960): 12.
120. Tom Hollingsworth used the quotation on evangelist Billy James Hargis's radio program, June 16, 1970, station KBYE, Oklahoma City.
121. *Dallas Morning News,* January 11, 1966; letter to Paul F. Boller, Jr., from Abraham Brumberg (ed.), *Problems of Communism,* February 28, 1966.
122. Kominsky, *Hoaxers,* 83–85.
123. Safire, "Sleeper Issue for the '88 Campaign: Child Care," *New York Times,* April 25, 1988, p. 23; Ezra Taft Benson, *An Enemy Hath Done This* (Salt Lake City, 1969), 229; *Hearings before a Subcommittee of the Committee on Appropriations, House of*

Representatives, 89th Congress, First Session, 316; Lenin, "The Tasks of the Youth Leagues," October 2, 1920, in Robert C. Tucker, *The Lenin Anthology* (New York, 1975), 665.

124. Brumberg, "Apropos of Quotation Mongering," 15.
125. *National Review,* I (November 19, 1955): 5.
126. Billy James Hargis, *The Far Left* (Tulsa, 1964), 7; Paul Horecky, Library of Congress, to John George, March 7, 1972; Julian Williams, Research Director, Christian Crusade, to John George, March 14, 1972.
127. Harry and Bonaro Overstreet, *The Strange Tactics of Extremism* (New York, 1968), 68–74; Karl E. Meyer, "The Elusive Lenin," *New York Times,* October 8, 1985, p. 26; "Excerpts from the Interview of Reagan by Soviet Journalists," *New York Times International,* May 29, 1988, p. 6.
128. Kominsky, *Hoaxers,* 27–35.
129. Brumberg, "Apropos of Quotation Mongering," 65; Douglass Cater, "Knowland: The Man Who Wants to Be Taft," *Reporter,* XIV (March 8, 1956): 32–35.
130. *In Fact,* November 14, 1949; May 15, 1950; *Congressional Record,* Volume 45, Part 9, 81st Congress, 1st Session, August 26, 1949, pp. 12344–45; Brumberg, "Apropos of Quotation Mongering," 15.
131. David Spitz, "The Timken Edition of Lenin," *Harper's Magazine,* CCXXII (March 1961): 56–57.
132. Fourteenth Report, Senate Investigating Committee on Education, Published by the Senate of the State of California, 1956 Budget Session, 25; from John Norpel to John George, June 23, 1970; from Gerald Hayward to John George, June 18, 1970.
133. "Strategy and Tactics of World Communism," Testimony of Nicholas T. Goncharoff before the Senate Internal Security Subcommittee, July 15, 1954, *Congressional Record,* Senate, p. 207.
134. V. I. Lenin, *Collected Works,* 45 vols. (Moscow, 1960–70), V, pp. 466–67.
135. Safire, "As Lenin May or May Not Have Said," *New York Times* News Service, April 29, 1987; letter to John George from Arnold Beichman, Hoover Institution, Stanford University, received, July 19, 1987; "Life After the Red Menace," *U.S. News & World Report,* December 21, 1987, p. 41.
136. "McCarthy, Hunt, and Facts Forum," *Reporter,* X (February 16, 1954): 27.
137. Albert A. Woldman, "Lincoln Never Said That," *Harper's Magazine,* CC (May 1950): 71–72; Seldes, *Great Quotations,* 123; Annual Message to Congress, December 3, 1861, *The Collected Works*

of *Abraham Lincoln*, 8 vols. (New Brunswick, N.J., 1953–55), V, p. 52.

138. *Il Popolo d'Italia*, April 2, 1920, p. 1; Richard H. Luthin, "Fakes and Frauds in Lincoln Literature," *Saturday Review*, XLII (February 14, 1959): 54.

139. Woldman, "Lincoln Never Said That," 72; Charles Chiniquy, *Fifty Years in the Church of Rome* (Chicago, 1886), 715; "Speech and Resolutions Concerning Philadelphia Riots," *Collected Works*, I, p. 338; Lincoln to Joshua Speed, August 24, 1855, *Collected Works*, II, p. 323.

140. Hugh T. Morrison, "Lincoln Didn't Say It," *Christian Century*, L (February 15, 1933): 229; Woldman, "Lincoln Never Said That," 73.

141. Woldman, "Lincoln Never Said That," 73–74.

142. Wills, *Reagan's America*, 143, 511.

143. Henry J. Taylor, "Still a Beacon for the Bewildered," United Features Syndicate, August 4, 1978; Clarence C. Macartney, *Lincoln and the Bible* (New York, 1949), mentions no such statement; nor does G. George Fox, *Abraham Lincoln's Religion* (New York, 1959).

144. Woldman, "Lincoln Never Said That," 73.

145. *New York Times*, February 13, 1954; "A 'Lincoln Hoax' Charged to G.O.P.," *Time*, LV (January 30, 1950): 58; Roy Basler, "What Did Lincoln Say?" *Abraham Lincoln Quarterly*, V (December 1949): 476–78.

146. George Seldes, *The Great Quotations* (New York, 1960), 21; James Morgan, *Our Presidents* (New York, 1928), 149.

147. Roy P. Basler, "Abe Between Quotes," *Saturday Review*, XXXIII (March 11, 1950): 12.

148. William E. Barton, *The Life of Abraham Lincoln*, 2 vols. (Indianapolis, 1925), II, pp. 367, 392; Luthin, "Fakes and Frauds in Lincoln Literature," 15; Basler, "Abe Between Quotes," 12.

149. "Text of Senator McCarthy's Speech Accusing Truman of Aiding Suspected Red Agent," *New York Times*, November 25, 1953, p. 5; "Speech at Edwardsville, Illinois," September 11, 1858, *Collected Works*, III, p. 95.

150. Chiniquy, *Fifty Years in Church of Rome*, 708; Fox, *Lincoln's Religion*, 52–53, 102–3; Lewis, *Myths after Lincoln*, 344–45.

151. Ludwell H. Johnson, "Lincoln and Equal Rights: The Authenticity of the Wadsworth Letter," *Journal of Southern History*, XXXII (February 1966): 83–86.

152. Woldman, "Lincoln Never Said That," 73–74

153. Ibid.

154. Frank W. Taussig, *Free Trade, the Tariff and Reciprocity* (New York, 1920), 34–43; Luthin, "Fakes and Frauds in Lincoln Literature," 16.
155. Lewis, *Myths after Lincoln*, 383–84; J. G. Holland, *Life of Abraham Lincoln* (Springfield, Mass., 1866), 237.
156. Lewis, *Myths after Lincoln*, 385–86; Fox, *Religion of Lincoln*, 72–73, taken from W. H. Herndon, *Abraham Lincoln* (Springfield, Mass., 1888), 442–46; William E. Barton, *The Soul of Abraham Lincoln* (New York, 1920), 208–9; see O. H. Oldroyd, *Words of Lincoln* (1883).
157. Emanuel Hertz, *Abraham Lincoln: A New Portrait*, 2 vols. (New York, 1931), II, p. 791; Luthin, "Fakes & Frauds in Lincoln Literature," 54.
158. Woldman, "Lincoln Never Said That," 73; "Fragment on Government," *Collected Works*, II, p. 220.
159. Woldman, "Lincoln Never Said That," 73–74.
160. Ibid.
161. John Remsburg, *Six Historic Americans* (New York, 1906), 211–13, 292; letter to John George from Illinois Senator Paul Simon, Lincoln specialist, March 29, 1985, enclosing negative results of research on the statement by Sarah Smith, Congressional Research Center, Library of Congress; letter to John George from Ralph G. Newman, Lincoln specialist, September 18, 1986, stating "there is no reliable reference to Lincoln's having made the statement"; *Collected Works*, VII, p. 542.
162. William Safire, "Here I Sit, No Warts at All," *New York Times Magazine*, March 6, 1988, pp. 18–20.
163. Woldman, "Lincoln Never Said That," 73.
164. Arthur Schlesinger, Jr., *The Politics of Upheaval* (Boston, 1960), 67, 664.
165. "Unlimited Credit," *Newsweek*, LXVII (February 7, 1966): 40.
166. Ibid.
167. Maurice Ashley, *Louis XIV and the Greatness of France* (New York, 1948), 21; John C. Rule (ed.), *Louis XIV and the Craft of Kingship* (Columbus, 1969), 233.
168. "New U.S. War Songs," *Life*, 13 (November 2, 1942): 43; Richardson, "They Didn't Say It," 39.
169. Philip Ressner, "God's Grace," *New York Times*, November 28, 1971, Section VII, p. 54; Bartlett, *Familiar Quotations*, 162.
170. Brumberg, "Apropos of Quotation Mongering," 15.
171. Richard Hanser, "Quotesmanship," *New York Times Magazine*,

August 10, 1980, p. 9; *The Confessions of Jean-Jacques Rousseau Newly Translated into English,* 2 vols. (Philadelphia and London, n.d.), I, p. 282.

172. The Truman quote and Groucho's denial are from memory. Groucho's friendly meeting with Truman appears in Groucho Marx and Richard J. Anobile, *The Marx Bros. Scrapbook* (New York, 1973), 206–7.

173. "Religious Tolerance, 17th-Century Style," *Reader's Digest,* XXXV (November 1939): 71; Curtis D. MacDougall, *New Hoaxes* (New York, 1941), 301.

174. Vincent Cronin, *Napoleon Bonaparte: An Intimate Biography* (New York, 1972), 211, 427, 467; J. Christopher Herold, *The Mind of Napoleon: A Selection from His Written and Spoken Words* (New York and London, 1955), 33. The Jesus-not-a-man statement appears in Hiram Casey (ed.), *Law, Love and Religion of Napoleon Bonaparte in His Own Words* (New York, 1961), 64; in Josh McDowell, *Evidence That Demands a Verdict: Historical Evidences for the Christian Faith* (San Bernardino, Calif., 1979), 106, 127, and elsewhere.

175. Philip Ward, *Dictionary of Common Fallacies* (New York, 1978), 172–73; Adam Smith, *An Inquiry into the Nature and Causes of the Wealth of Nations,* ed. Edwin Cannon (New York, 1937), 579.

176. Burnham, *Dictionary of Misinformation,* 224–25.

177. Robert K. Merton, *On the Shoulders of Giants: A Shandean Postscript* (New York, 1965), 1–13.

178. John H. Taylor, "Nixon at the Wall," *New York Times,* September 18, 1987, p. 30.

179. Flo Conway and Jim Siegelman, *Holy Terror* (New York, 1982), 237–39; Bob E. Mathews, "Gullible People Easily Hoodwinked," *The Baptist Messenger,* June 6, 1985; "Letters of Hate," *New York Times,* April 14, 1988, p. B6.

180. Hanser, "Of Deathless Remarks," 55.

181. *Writings of Paine,* 10 vols. (New York, 1915), VI, p. 98.

182. Major W. P. Drury (William Price), *The Tadpole of an Archangel: The Petrified Eye and Other Naval Stories* (London, 1904), x; Rosenblum. "They Never Said It," 497.

183. John J. Pershing, *My Experiences in the World War,* 2 vols. (New York, 1931), I, p. 93.

184. James M. Markham, "The Bad Pétain Haunts the Good One," *New York Times,* February 11, 1988, p. 4; Richardson, "They Didn't Say It," 39; Hanser, "Of Deathless Remarks," 58.

185. E. N. Sanctuary, "Exposure of the Franklin 'Prophecy'" (unpublished, 1943), Wilcox Collection, University of Kansas, Lawrence.
186. Stefan Lorant, *The Glorious Burden: The American Presidency* (New York, 1968), 53–54; Henry F. Woods, *American Sayings* (New York, 1945), 13; Hanser, "Of Deathless Remarks," 55; Sid Moody, Associated Press, "History Has a Way of Bending Quotes," *Fort Worth Star-Telegram*, May 11, 1986, p. AA1.
187. Burnham, *Dictionary of Misinformation*, 69–70.
188. Albert Chandler, *The Clash of Political Ideals* (New York, 1957), 190–91; David Bell, "The Jews Left Behind," *New Republic*, 192 (February 18, 1985): 12–14; Kenneth Jacobson, *The Protocols: Myth and History* (New York, 1981); Albert Lee, *Henry Ford and the Jews* (New York, 1980).
189. "A Rabbi Speaks: Foretells Gentile Doom," *Common Sense*, VI (August 1, 1952): 1; Frank P. Mintz, *The Liberty Lobby and the American Right* (Westport, Conn., 1985), 59.
190. "A Rabbi Speaks," 1; *The Independent*, January 1958, p. 1.
191. "Images," *Time*, 130 (December 28, 1987): 52; "Letters,"*Time*, 130 (January 18, 1988): 7.
192. *New York Post*, April 12, 1988, p. 5; *New York Times*, April 13, 1988, p. A16; Michael Kinsley, "Unspeakable," *Washington Post*, April 14, 1988, p. A23; *New York Times*, April 14, 1988, p. A34; *Washington Post*, April 14, 1988, p. A3; William Raspberry, "Speakes' Worst Offense," *Washington Post*, April 15, 1988, p. A19; *New York Times*, April 21, 1988, p. 14; *Houston Post*, April 20, 1988, p. 2A.
193. *The Autobiography of Lincoln Steffens* (New York, 1931), 799.
194. Robert W. Smith, "A Package of Political Poison," *Minneapolis Tribune*, September 20, 1964, reprinted, *Christian Century*, LXXXI (October 14, 1964): 1263–64; Robert F. Kennedy, *The Enemy Within* (New York, 1960), 295–96; John George telephone conversation with Victor Reuther, October 12, 1985.
195. Homer Croy, *Our Will Rogers* (New York, 1953), 286–88.
196. See Mark Twain.
197. Hanser, "Of Deathless Remarks," 58.
198. Julian Foster, "None Dare Call It Reason: A Critique of John Stormer's 'None Dare Call It Treason'" (Placentia, California, 1964); Bruce Galphin, "Pop Literature of the Radical Right," *New Republic*, CLI (October 10, 1964): 24; Fred Cook, *The FBI Nobody Knows* (New York, 1964), 240–43.
199. Donald Janson, "Communist Rules for Revolt Viewed as Durable

Fraud," *New York Times*, July 10, 1970, p. 1, 30; "Communist Rules for Revolution" *Congressional Record*, Vol. 115, Part 18, 91st Congress, 1st Session, August 13, 1969, pp. 23697–99; Dennis L. Cuddy, Senior Associate, National Council on Educational Research, "Basic Traditional Values," *Fort Worth Star-Telegram*, June 26, 1986, p. A15, accepted it as authentic.

200. David Wellechinsky, *The Complete Book of the Olympics* (New York, 1984), 13.
201. Richardson, "They Didn't Say It," 39.
202. St. John Ervine, *Bernard Shaw: His Life, Work and Friends* (New York, 1956), 531–32; Hesketh Pearson, *G.B.S.: A Full Length Portrait and a Postscript* (New York, 1942, 1950), 366.
203. Zierold, *Moguls*, 128.
204. Paul Andrew Hutton, *Phil Sheridan and His Army* (Lincoln, Neb., 1985), 180–81.
205. Lloyd Lewis, *Sherman: Fighting Prophet* (New York, 1932), 426.
206. Lewis, *Sherman*, 235, 636; Hanser, "Of Deathless Remarks," 56.
207. *Daily Oklahoman*, October 20 1970; *Oklahoma Journal*, November 30, 1970; *The Councilor* (Citizens Councils Publication, Shreveport, La.), November 1978, p. 14; Josef Stalin, *Marxism and the National and Colonial Question* (New York, 1942), 116.
208. Richard F. Gibbons, "Whose Eggs?," *New York Times*, April 7, 1957, Section VI, p. 6, commenting on Flora Lewis's "Poland's Gomulka Walks a Tightrope," March 24, 1957, in which she calls it a "Communist adage." Gibbons notes that Stevenson, *Home Book of Proverbs, Maxims and Familiar Phrases*, credits the epigram to Robespierre in 1790.
209. "Enter the Sword: The Real Reasons Why Communism Will Soon Swallow Up America," *Christ Is All*, Box 490, Vernon, Alabama, p. 1.
210. Kominsky, *Hoaxers*, 499–504.
211. Burnham, *More Misinformation*, 130.
212. Foster, "None Dare Call It Reason"; Robert A. Taft, *A Foreign Policy for America* (New York, 1951), 37.
213. Roy, *Apostles of Discord*, 38.
214. Alexis de Tocqueville, *Democracy in America*, 2 vols., ed. Phillips Bradley (New York, 1953), I, p. 191.
215. Hanser, "Quotesmanship," 10.
216. Ibid.
217. *The Autobiography of Mark Twain*, ed., Charles Neider (New York, 1959), 149.

218. *Mark Twain's Autobiography*, 2 vols., with introduction by Albert Bigelow Paine (New York, 1924), I, p. 338.
219. Hanser, "Quotesmanship," 10; "Warner Said It," *Wilson Library Bulletin*, XV (February 1941): 515.
220. S. G. Tallentyre, *The Friends of Voltaire* (London, 1906), 176–205; William Rose Benét, "Phoenix Nest," *Saturday Review of Literature*, XXX (May 10, 1947): 35; (June 28, 1947): 36; and (August 2, 1947): 22.
221. Kominsky, *Hoaxers*, 15–17; Paul F. Boller, Jr., *George Washington and Religion* (Dallas, 1963), 186–87.
222. Boller, *Washington and Religion*, 39–41; "Proposed Address to Congress," April 1789, *The Writings of George Washington*, 38 vols. (Washington, 1931–44), XXX, pp. 301–2.
223. Mason L. Weems, *The Life of Washington*, 1809 ed., ed. Marcus Conliffe (Cambridge, Mass., 1962) 12.
224. "Budget Must Be Balanced," *Daily Oklahoman,* March 7, 1988, p. 6.
225. Henry J. Taylor, "Still a Beacon for the Bewildered," United Features Syndicate, August 5, 1978, used the Bible quote. A good account of Washington's last hours appears in James Thomas Flexner, *George Washington: Anguish and Farewell, 1793–1799* (Boston, 1969, 1972), 460.
226. Woodrow Wilson, *George Washington* (New York, 1896), 229; Boller, *Washington and Religion,* 6.
227. *Treaties, Conventions, International Acts, Protocols and Agreements between the United States of America and Other Powers,* 4 vols. (Washington, 1910–38), II, p. 1786.
228. Sir Herbert Maxwell, *The Life of Wellington*, 2 vols. (Boston, 1899), II, p. 82.
229. Elizabeth Longford, *Wellington: The Years of the Sword* (New York, 1969), 16–17.
230. Russell Baker, "For the Love of Error," *New York Times*, January 11, 1986, p. 17.
231. William S. Baring Gould, *The Lure of the Limerick: An Uninhibited History* (New York, 1967), 83; Arthur S. Link to Laurence Perrine, April 23, 1985.
232. "George Lincoln Rockwell: Playboy Interview," *Playboy*, April 1966, p 79.
233. Burnham, *More Misinformation*, 128.
234. Brian Crozier to John George, September 26, 1985; Ross Terrill to John George, November 22, 1985; Irene Schubert to Senator David Boren, from the Congressional Research Service, Library of Congress, late in 1985; John George's conversation with Fox

Butterfield, *New York Times* correspondent formerly in China, November 16, 1987; Mohamed Heikal, *Nasser: The Cairo Documents* (New York, 1972), 277–78.

235. Paul W. Blackstock, *Agents of Deceit: Frauds, Forgeries and Political Intrigues among Nations* (Chicago, 1966), 81–102; *New York Times*, December 19, 20, 1923.

Index